CRITICS WHO KNOW JACK
URBAN MYTHS, MEDIA AND ROCK & ROLL

ESSENTIAL ESSAYS SERIES 62

Canada Council   Conseil des Arts
for the Arts   du Canada

ONTARIO ARTS COUNCIL
CONSEIL DES ARTS DE L'ONTARIO

50 YEARS OF ONTARIO GOVERNMENT SUPPORT OF THE ARTS
50 ANS DE SOUTIEN DU GOUVERNEMENT DE L'ONTARIO AUX ARTS

Guernica Editions Inc. acknowledges the support of the Canada Council
for the Arts and the Ontario Arts Council. The Ontario Arts Council
is an agency of the Government of Ontario.

We acknowledge the financial support of the Government of Canada
through the Canada Book Fund (CBF) for our publishing activities.

CRITICS WHO KNOW JACK
URBAN MYTHS, MEDIA AND ROCK & ROLL

Joseph Maviglia

GUERNICA

TORONTO • BUFFALO • BERKELEY• LANCASTER (U.K.)

2014

Michael Mirolla, editor
David Moratto, interior book design
Guernica Editions Inc.
P.O. Box 76080, Abbey Market, Oakville, (ON), Canada L6M 3H5
2250 Military Road, Tonawanda, N.Y. 14150-6000 U.S.A.

Distributors:
University of Toronto Press Distribution,
5201 Dufferin Street, Toronto (ON), Canada M3H 5T8
Gazelle Book Services, White Cross Mills, High Town, Lancaster LA1 4XS U.K.

First edition.
Printed in Canada.

Legal Deposit—First Quarter
Library of Congress Catalog Card Number: 2013953833
Library and Archives Canada Cataloguing in Publication
Maviglia, Joseph, 1953-, author
Critics who know Jack : urban myths,
media and rock & roll / Joseph Maviglia.

(Essential essays series ; 62)
Essays.
Issued in print and electronic formats.
ISBN 978-1-55071-837-9 (pbk.).--ISBN 978-1-55071-838-6 (epub).--
ISBN 978-1-55071-839-3 (mobi)

I. Title. II. Series: Essential essays series (Toronto, Ont.) ; 62

PS8576.A8576C75 2014   C814'.54   C2013-907533-X   C2013-907534-8

Thanks and love to all!

'I don't really wanna stop the show
but I thought you'd all like to know
that the singer's gonna sing a song
and he wants you all to sing along...'
—Lennon and McCartney

CONTENTS

PREFACE

*I*ntroductions are never easy. I remember the last time I met a woman I came to spend a few years with. A friend who was attending an event with me called me over, saying there was someone I should meet. I was busy with the antipasto and wine and my hand was getting fairly oily from the sun-dried tomatoes. In any case, I rushed over to my friend's side and he said: "This is _____." And before I could wipe my hand down on a superbly inefficient mini-napkin, there it was. Oil all over her right palm though I had tried in earnest to lose the oil in a couple of hand shakes leading up to that sort of fateful hand-shake.

Introductions are never easy. Read any introduction to a translation of Dante's Divine Comedy and you will feel nausea (unless maybe you wrote it). I prefer liner notes. Like you would find on old vinyl 33 and 1/3rd long-playing record covers. Or compact disc collections. Though I preferred *the print size on the albums. Liner notes don't seem to go on too long. And they are (were) always enhanced by visuals. You don't tend to get that with books. Sure, there are illustrated books and comics and graphic novels but texts per se rarely have visual introductions. So try and visualize this.*

A set of titles coming in early one spring morning. Walking along in the chilly April air and titles coming like lines in a poem. Tumbling in one after another after days of reading, watching TV news and DVDs. Listening to CDs. Playing guitar and walking to parks on the way to cafes or walking to cafes on the way back from parks. Dodging dogs and their leashes. Moving my foot out of the way from an on-coming pram. Remembering MAD *magazine and running the neighbourhood streets with my older brother. Getting a song on a Juno Award-winning CD compilation. Being asked to play a song I dedicated to my father for his retirement for the umpteenth time. Watching the umpires tolerate the shenanigans of Major League Baseball players. Digging Coltrane as I turn down the volume on World Cup Soccer. Spending time in a cabin in the woods. Watching a snake slither down a tree and then up again (no apples in sight) and shed its skin.*

Think of a day that doesn't exist. Out of time. June 31st, 7 o'clock in the afternoon. When to write the titles out into segments. Think semiotics and Marshall McLuhan. Think of the last time a critic for any medium sat like a fat calf expert, collecting his or her wage for the weekly column while an artist waits on grant submission replies and eats dark bread for protein. Read Dylan Thomas, Walt Whitman, Dante, Auden, Ginsberg and The New York Times *again and again. Listen to everything from Leadbelly to Paul Robeson. Then Zimmerman Bob and BRUUUCE and Lennon and meet a woman who wants to sleep in a "tantric" sort of way and whisper "unlunar" incantations (apologies to T.S. Eliot). Dig the moon landing and the radical nature of the New Left circa 1968.*

Meet another woman who works as a therapist but is into conspiracy theory. Visit the "pining" west coast of Canada. Read MAD *magazine again. Have more great espresso and try not to spit out the bad ones in public. Go to the cabin in the woods again. Go because you can't be online and there is no service provider but with your fingers on a portable typewriter, letting your grade ten fingers tap the night away against the glow of candles and kerosene lamps. Shave by moonlight and think of Warren Zevon's* Werewolves of London *then* The Clash's London Calling.

Get back to the city and rent all the available episodes of The Fugitive *in black and white and don't pay attention to federal election results. Play a couple of club concerts and run home and try to visualize what a text on all this would run like. Feel ornery because the personal computer gives off too much light and underlines your whole text in red and green. Be grateful that when you write poems or songs on your PC you use caesuras and the PC doesn't know how to underline them. See all the artists in the neighbourhood in beachcomber slacks and Frank Sinatra hats, gawking at the well-toned Victorian houses and whisper how they got to get one.*

Dig French, Italian and Spanish radio programming. It seems only the English stations have mile long ads. Re-watch the moon landing of nineteen-sixty-nine. Have more espresso. Try and follow the lines on the latest tattoos on folks in the neighbourhood and think sailors and Moby Dick's "cannibal" Queequeg and bad CSI programs where the technology acts better than the actors (including actresses). They are bad in both genders. Avoid the annual Film Festival at all costs 'cause it costs too much! Chase down the ice-cream truck where a cone costs a dollar and half compared to the three dollars and fifty cents it costs for a badly made gelato. Eat hazelnuts instead. Visit organic markets and grow tomatoes and eggplants. Only withdraw enough money from your ATM each day and not enough for a week 'cause you will spend it all in a day. Leave your bank card at home after you do and let your credit card sit tucked and warm in your wallet at home next to your passport for a real decent other country getaway.

• • •

A flock of starlings has just flown over the cabin. Here, deep in the woods, they all sing the same song. All look the same. Probably have names only they know to themselves but in ways we have trouble understanding. And they flock from tree to tree and whoosh up in unison, scattering a few autumnal leaves about, casting a buzz into the late afternoon air. I am lucky, I say. This was not a show I knew anything about. I didn't have a dial or remote to check out what was on. Didn't even have a TV on to tell of the coming feathered friends. Totemists must have an answer for this. Thousands of black starlings must mean something more than migration and, if only migration, that must mean something. This is way beyond espresso and may require a good scotch or grappa! I sip and frolic in their frolic. This is paradise and there are no apples except for a few I picked up on the ride in.

Punctuation and happiness! Exact winds twirling the leaves up and down and bringing on the clouds and rain! Ecstasy! In the beginning there was no apple and no worm! No serpent and no William Jennings Bryan. Nor Clarence Darrow. There may have been Dharma *and the self-referential wallowing of cooing doves. The attraction without apples and parentheses that crept up on us like a good landscape will. At times we are convalescing. At times we thrive! May our dreams be vigorous with peace and stretched-out in the morning across open plains. No heed and no redemption. Live in amaze and hum in bliss!*

Introductions are never easy. The stage awaits. It's time for sound-check.

THE FUGITIVE

(TV Program)

D avid Jansen — *Richard Kimble* — always running — a
man of health (a doctor) and his future is a question and in turn, day to day, a quest. He fights
against injustice first personally and then professionally as a doctor
— he has taken "oaths" to care for those that require healing — a
healing most distinct — the healing of others' projected morality.
And those that wait in the unconscious valley of their fears have
the choice to turn him in or raise their souls to a humanity and
humility rarely seen in latter day dramas. Where the pursued is
definitely of evil sensibility and the pursuit of the criminal is cast
in "black and white." Raising our need to blame regardless of the
corruption of our senses. Our honour and our "biblicality," our
popular beliefs about ourselves as individuals, yet citizens. This

"constant" drives the pain of false accusation that Kimble faces episode to episode into our afterimage day to day. For if we accept the reality of the series' "noirishness," we go to bed (or went to bed) thinking of his sins and in turn our sins and those of others we were quick to accuse. This sense of accusation. Of making black and white of the troubles Kimble faces, and the pursuit of him by Lt. Gerard, brings our comforts and our fears to light.

We in turn find ourselves superior and then somehow touch a sense of what we have done wrong that we would wish forgiveness for. Our sympathies and compassion go to bed with us after each episode and we wake to the day, thinking of how fortunate we are that no one is pursuing us for truth except the taxman and death. And perhaps the government and our wives or husbands, sisters, brothers, fathers, mothers, friends and relations may have something on us. Yet they may also fear we have something on them. Maybe not murder but something smaller (for we are not in the direct drama). Only the indirect one, and mistily, unknowingly, as it is always night which fascinates us most with Kimble and the darkness of his initial escape (though he has many). Rarely does he escape during the day. Thus he runs in our dreams.

In these dreams we have repercussions and obsessions and manner of right and wrong. Are forced to make do until the next morning arrives full of rave and comfort, civility and privacy. We do not expect to be encroached upon for matters that are not our affairs. Nor do we like it. We do not practice provocation to assault the boundaries of others' trials and tribulations but for incidents of fate and coincidence. Richard Kimble symbolizes a time in America (and perhaps other parts of the developed world) where the unwritten code of giving a stranger a hand was still in practice in the post-World War II era when *The Fugitive* was telecast. The country was still considerably rural and morality was uncompli- cated. Wheat grew upwards from the ground as long as there was rain and sun.

In the "days of Kimble," governments were not generally perceived by the public as corrupt entities. The period of 1962 to 1966 was a period of growth and prosperity, and in turn, trust for most of America. Or at least, the aspiration towards a good, honourable life was in the air. Kimble was the great American loner. Forced to be by circumstance. His appeal to us was that he was able to wander, change jobs, meet other women (or men), see the country and the city (albeit through the constant fear of capture). Inventiveness, tenacity and courage added to his Hippocratic oath. Gave him a mantle through which we could see the foibles and honour in our system of morality. We were asked indirectly: *What would you do in Kimble's situation? Would we want the benefit of the doubt? Would we want ourselves turned in if we knew we had not done wrong?* And further: *Was it our civic duty (Lt. Gerard) to turn him in or could we judge situations for ourselves and substantiate our capacity for reasoning and critical thinking and a sense of judgment not dependent on the courts of law?*

Richard Kimble's moments of grace came from his actions (this being the ingenuity of his creators). To create adventure and through that adventure have us as viewers possibly philosophize and moralize in witness to his behaviour. We could at once "be him" and then "be other"—other being a good citizen and turn him in? Or an understanding citizen and help him hide or escape? A runner from false accusation or simply William Conrad's narrative voice of stark reality, sub-textually saying: *Look at the horror this man faces day to day while you cut your front lawn and trim the hedges and go on vacation.*

The remake or film version starring Harrison Ford cast Kimble further along into the twentieth century (the nineteen-nineties). It is noteworthy that the character as interpreted by Ford moved day to day with fear and a sense of being wronged but rarely did his performance show the subtlety of Jansen through humility and slight movement of eye or lips and awkwardness as though written by Franz Kafka. Ford's performance was fear and a sense of revenge towards the one-armed man for having made his life difficult. Jansen's pursuit of the one-armed man was not vengeance but a desire for relief and a return to normalcy. Ford's performance was more superficial. Ironically a more "black and white" representation of Kimble's core.

In short, the story was as important as the character in Jansen's version. As a weekly series, he had the advantage of developing the character over the period of six years whereas Ford had a one time (two hour) shot at Kimble. And the "neatness" of presentation by the TV producers and directors, giving us four acts and an "epilog" suggested to us theatre and tragedy and possible resolution to the circumstances Kimble faced. Even as commercial breaks came along, you had the drama brought to a sense of crescendo by the dominant musical score beginning and ending each "Act."

The period *The Fugitive* was created and filmed in must be stressed here. Early mid-60s America was a time of liberalism coming out after a fear-driven 1950s. The rebel was more than revered through the performances of Marlon Brando and James Dean, and the films about marginalized characters directed by Elia Kazan. The music of the time and culture at large found determined concern with civil rights and non-conformity. By design Kimble was in some ways "the outsider" of Camus. The rebel of the times though he did come from the establishment (a doctor) to begin with. And he was Kerouac's Sal Paradise on the road and also a Hemingway/Faulkner-type protagonist. Almost at times righting wrongs by his movement to claim his prior life. But he was not the rebel of provocation and causelessness. He was driven by a personal sense of freedom from false accusation and in turn, became an *anti*-anti-hero. He chased bikers and carried some of the Republican John Wayne in him, balanced by being *forced* (by necessity not pleasure) "onto" the road.

THE SPIRIT OF ABBIE HOFFMAN

The ultimate American rebel! Make that American shit disturber to many! Instigator — provocateur — athlete — media hip — manic depressive — fighter for justice — street-smart and well-educated — Abbie Hoffman was the best known American rebel since the agents of The Boston Tea Party and Confederate General Robert E. Lee. Hoffman, having grown up in Worcester, Massachusetts and attending Brandeis University (the hotbed of Jewish-American intellectualism and liberal thought), spent his early years trying to make it in small business (and with girls), wrestling through high school and trying to out-smart the next street hustler (with whom he found kinship) as the politics of civil rights and anti-establishment sentiment grew on the horizon.

So what did it take to be a citizen of America in the 1960s to mid-1970s compared to today? One distinct current was an age differential between World War Two parents and their offspring, whereas the movements of 2008 and even the 1990s saw the generations of the '60s and '70s become the "older" generation. Wars (as in Vietnam) existed as do wars today (Afghanistan and Iraq). What changed? What would make a man with the political and street theatre chops of Abbie Hoffman be the odd man out in today's America? Or would he be? Is the current again changing to a counter-establishment premise? And what would Abbie, an American Jew, make of or feel about the Arab-Israeli conflict and the incursions on civil liberties many Arab and Muslim Americans (and other citizens) face within the Babylon of the war against terror?

Hoffman's radicalism was no doubt more authentic compared to the posed rock & roll "stance" of, say, The Rolling Stones. Perhaps closer to the essence of Thoreau and Whitman mixed in with Allen Ginsberg and the Beat writers, and the Jewish-American tradition of 1930s socialism, he finds his channelling?—what he drew from to expose America's fascistic tendencies. What makes a man get arrested time and time again for saying: *Stop the War!?*

What makes a man turn cartwheels after his arrest while protesting the capitalist establishment of the New York Stock Exchange and throw dollar bills down from the gallery to the men in suits and ties below? Could it be Abbie was thinking of the poem by W.H. Auden where, in honour of W.B. Yeats, he says:

> *And when the Frenchmen are roaring like*
> *beasts on the floor of the Bourse . . . some one will remember this*
> *day . . .*

Revolution was not just for the hell of it as Abbie said—and yet he did make it fun. The generation he grew up in allowed for fun.

Yes fun! Even in revolution! The media allowed for it. The play of visual and the lights of television screens made revolution something you could see day to day. Add to that the joy and explosive nature of the "new" rock & roll and its never-ending exploration of the subconscious coming to the surface in chrysalises of expression both musical and word-ly — and you have something to invest in as a youth movement. A great sense of space for "fun" not to be ruined by the greed of war and un-required disciplines from earlier (post WW2) times.

Spoils? Spending a lifetime on the run for standing up to the lies of the country's leaders is hardly a manifestation of living the spoiled life. Master of Agit-Prop and street theatre, Hoffman knew how to create a character that was both outspoken and to address the political issues of the day through a complex consideration of "sign and symbol." He knew the *semiotics* of effect and the nature of the American media. Fickle for a storyline that showed the counter-culture as unruly, long-haired and "un-American." Hoffman played off this media need brilliantly time and time again. He became the darling of the "radical chic" and in truth was offered substantial contracts to become a television icon and fashion gadfly for the commercial enterprises wanting to take full advantage of the "youth dollars" the generation was born into. His American-flag shirt was replicated again and again (similar yet more political than Peter Townshend's of The Who, and his Union-Jack jacket). This proved Hoffman's great sense of the theatric that the press and commercial interests were eager to pursue and cash in on.

To be defiant was cool and hip yet underlying this "attractive" stance, Hoffman had political chops: a substantial activism based on socialist and other left-leaning ideological frameworks. The freshness or the newness of his antics was in great part the result of the time he lived and "worked" in. The explosion of media and television. The rush to culture by a high percentage of Americans both young and old. Yet with Abbie, it did not stop at symbol. Risking his life, he and many other young Americans pushed Lyndon Johnson from the White House and helped end the Vietnam War through constant exposure of the hypocrisy and aggressive actions of the State. And with Richard Nixon's paranoid presidency, demonstrations that swayed public and world opinion contributed to exposing Nixon's larceny-driven morality and his eventual demise.

Hoffman committed suicide after years of being on the run. He had plastic surgery to change his well-known features and continued his activism even as a bipolar disorder consumed his once agile and clear, loving mind. Certainly if Abbie were around today he would be yelling: *Steal This iPad!* He made a forceful difference in American politics and culture and its says something that the country he was born in never found a way to honour his contrarianism and citizenry, as much as it seems to love its rebels and sense of integrity.

The Artist as Homeowner, Or: *Bring Me Two Capps!*

A film-maker in the neighbourhood I live in is always looking for the next good idea for an independent film and how to buy a house at the same time. His real work is doing some post-editing for bigger productions and a few hours a week in a bookstore as a clerk that allows him some part time to pursue his higher interest. His wife could have been a model but applies her congeniality to being a cultural administrator's receptionist. Yet they struggle. Day to day they are seen morning, noon and evening consuming lattes and watching every new face that comes into the neighbourhood cafes. Their interest in meeting people has everything to do with: *Who will be the next person who might be the light at the end of the tunnel?* The great breakthrough person who will present an opportunity and moment that will raise their profile and light? And get them off the "poor end" of the café stools? Their eyes are on the door constantly.

Rents are high in the neighbourhood and home ownership near impossible unless a parent or a relative with saved funds passes on. So there they wait. Though if you look around the length of the café, you will see them in double and triplicate. All resentful of each others' position and, at the same time, encroachment on each others' space.

This is where their quest for culture has put them. Full of envy and connivance. Superficial and fatigued in their struggle. Embarrassed that as they age they can no longer "afford" that extra dollar to put in the local street-person's cup. Taking the other side of the street to avoid him and cringing as he calls out: *How are ya? Have a good day!*

The home they want? An old three-story Victorian with a garden and sunroof. A room for him to film edit and a room for her to practice the painting class assignments she takes at the local high school. Long wooden pine tables for guests and Christmases and Easters and a finished basement they can rent to an arts student to help pay the mortgage.

This all steams away in them. This dream of ownership under the espresso machines of Joe, Tony and Frank, giving them the caffeine runs while their fairly insecure employment awaits them every morning.

They are not Old Testament Job. They would rather others suffered and haven't been near a church since last year's Passion Procession where he had the idea to film old country folks mourning away in their past and present beliefs.

The price of the Victorian of their dreams is no less than seven-hundred-thousand dollars. They have little saved. They're growing older. They're more and more grumpy as each day passes them by. They're in that limbo between the energized skin of their youth and the doom of walkers and old folks' homes they have not prepared for.

What to do? The old folks are dying and haven't saved a dime. "Two capps, Tony! Make 'em extra strong!"

BAD POP SONGS

Every era has its kitsch. And every era its spectrum of popular song that ranges from the facile and trite to the higher forms of contemporary composition. And every era seems to introduce a new medium. From Victrolas to mp3s and all in between. And every song is subject to interpretation. One most noteworthy being *Mack the Knife* (originally *Die Moritat von Mackie Messer*), part of German playwright Bertolt Brecht's *Threepenny Opera*. Music by Kurt Weill; lyrics by Brecht himself.

The song, written in the voice of a narrator, speaks of Macheath (Mack the Knife), all around gangster, bad guy, *voyou*, playboy, hustler, murderer and superiorly masterful underground liver in the shadows of 1920s and '30s Berlin. He represents cunning and throat-cutting. A king of the underworld and underclass. Marginal yet prince and thief, who rules by his "own sword" (slash) KNIFE. The song's treatment was presented in the course of theatrical performance and worked as Brecht's dark characterization of the vast underworld created by socio-economic upheaval and uncertainty. Macheath did not come from riches and, unlike Robin of Sherwood, he not only robbed from the rich but from the poor as well.

Move forward to 1960 USA. Bobby Darin—'50s rock idol cum Vegas lounge-king—decides to take this intensely political song and render it with trumpets and a big band sound in an almost self-representational deprecation and laurelling, and spank it onto the American music charts. In Darin's version the wickedness of Macheath is oiled up into a crescendo of suave pseudo-hip, Rat-packy, coolest-man-in-town, with all the babes lining up stylization. *The line forms on the right, Babe, now that Mackie's back in town* sings Darin as though his metaphoric lady-killing is being awaited by every female within range of his cologne. This is not the stench and filth of early twentieth century Berlin. Nor is it a conscious reverence of a vile character by Darin. From the viewpoint of "sign and symbol," culturally it is a violation and corruption of a vastly important articulation on underclass culture that Brecht's Marxism intended in his original penning of the lyric.

Now the Bad Pop Song/Good Pop Song part. With formulaic interception of the song's meaning, Darin created an arrangement that was pleasing to the American listening public. Like many other singers of his time, Darin found novelty in foreign-language songs that the American market had not been exposed to en masse. Note here in the same period *Danke Schein* by Wayne Newton and Elvis Presley's version of the pastoral Neapolitan *O Sole Mio* transposed as *It's Now or Never*. While those songs were somewhat innocent in their adaptation, the Darin version of Brecht's *Knife* corrupted the meaning and intent from the original's socialist perspective to syrup-ing in the false gods and golden fat-calves of Las Vegas.

Darin completely guts the song's meaning to mere shank, though Vegas itself was built by an underclass from New York and New Jersey. The underclass or underworld of Italian and Jewish American 20th century mobsterism. And in truth, Brecht was fascinated by the American Mobster and corruption by capitalist enterprise. Yet he *did not celebrate it as a way to be.* His play *The Resistible Rise of Arturo Ui*, in which metaphoric character associations are made between Hitler' Reich and Chicago's 1930s gangsterism, is one of the great social condemnations of greed in modern theatre. However none of this information seems to have informed Darin. There is no satire nor irony in Darin's adaptation. It is all joy and grease.

As a footnote, American folk-singer Dave Van Ronk did record a version of Brecht and Weill's song with an integrity and fear that would have made Brecht smile. In Van Ronk's version (in English) each verse rises with the sharp edge of a blade. Van Ronk's vocal cutting to a peak and slash and slaughter by song's end. This version is not pop song and has no pretension to be so. For the most part being limited to the esoteric world of independent record production. Though its artistic merit sits high in the pantheon of recorded music. In turn, is Darin's *Mack the Knife* a bad pop song? In its triteness and treatment of subject matter? Considering the song's origin, it is. As an American hit of the period one thanks the god of pop music that the Beatles and Bob Dylan were more than establishing artistic stronghold on the American charts, giving us great alternatives to schmaltz and lounge-lizardry.

BAD ESPRESSO

In Rome, *il guaglione* (the young punk) behind the counter turns a line in a cappuccino preparation and lifts the deep brown espresso to the surface foam into a heart for the young Japanese traveller. He has not cashed in money from her and his eye is already on the door, setting two espresso cups out for his next customers. She sips lightly on her cappuccino, careful not to let her lips break the heart the barista has designed. She smiles and he returns it. He sets the two other espressos out for the well-suited bureaucrats who have made their early morning pilgrimage here before heading into the city's financial district for a day's work of accounting and paper-shuffling.

Over the course of the next half hour seven more customers have come into the café and the young man has served each their coffee without waiting for a cue as to what they desire. But for the Japanese student, they are regulars and have not lined up behind each other or paid for their drinks before being served. This is not Starbuck's pretending charm and pseudo-Feng Shui with its cardboard cut outs of Kenyan mountains and Colombian bean-growers with straw hats and moustaches—and its over-priced caramelized coffee beans! Its counter people and baristas rattling in the cost of your beverage and waiting for your money as they call out the drink to another worker who is busy changing the satellite radio station to annoying high-pitched boy-band music. With all of this, the espresso you order is made from a touch of a button and thin as watered maple syrup. And what seems to elude the Starbuck's chain is the wonder of viscosity (what happens when you steam coffee and milk and water together for that delightful weighted foam or *crema* (the golden brown top of a properly steamed espresso).

You ask if they can remake it and they are happy to do it again and are apologetic and it comes out much the same. This time you frown at the meagre and thin portion and go to the plastic sticks and cream counter and add extra cream to at least tolerate the bitter taste. And, of course, you add a touch of sugar, which is brown as if you are at least practicing something healthy regardless of how badly the coffee is "prepared."

And you have taken the time to tell them how it is done in Roman cafes and one of them says: *Cool. I was there last summer with my folks but not all the time.* And you ask: *Doing what?* And he says: *I'm studying here at the College of Art and Design* And you say to yourself: *This is not Caravaggio making my espresso this morning. Not even Gauguin. He would probably have spit the first taste out. Yet if he had a patron he wouldn't have been paying for it so maybe he'd just be looking forward to getting back to his studio and whipping down a hardy grappa or half litre of red.* But the young Roman barista knew you were in the land of Caravaggio and even if he slips once or twice and makes an inferior brew, you at least are taken by the aura of it all and go out and sulk by a Roman ruin as opposed to resenting that you ever stopped at Starbuck's expecting a decent and simple beginning to your morning.

Take then your fine Roman espresso and walk along the Tiber to Trastevere in autumn and think of the Argentine steakhouse near Via Cavour that you will dine at this evening (with a full Tango ensemble) and let fade the snotty little vegan muffin shop where a cup of milk is rarely available and if asked for, a glance of damnation sits stupidly on the face of the anaemic unwashed third-generation, twenty-something counter person, back in the North country, across the Atlantic. You could be here in Rome if you just made your own stove top espresso or cappuccino at home and saved five dollars latte money every day for a year. *Caravaggio awaits you!*

GREAT POP SONGS

We all have our own personal top ten. Name yours? Here's my list but not in order, as no order exists for them. Instead, they sit side by side in a sort of forever-ness while other songs (mostly good) satellite around this Milky Way.

Won't Get Fooled Again, written by Pete Townshend for The Who. To underline how great this song is, I knew a kid back in first year university that couldn't get to sleep at night unless he had this song playing full-blast through his headphones. He aced his French and Math exams the next week as long as Roger Daltrey's voice ran through his membrane and engaged his Circle of Willis, establishing the anatomical purpose of the blood-brain barrier.

La Bamba, by Richie Valens. One of the first runs at what came to be known as Tex-Mex, later Conjunto and Tejeno, and years before the World Music craze of the 1990s, *La Bamba* was adapted by the 17-year-old Valens (Valenzuela) from a Mexican folk song into a rockabilly, Buddy Holly-like wailing rhythm, breath-taking arpeggio guitar solo and lyrics all in Spanish. The Chicano had arrived on the music scene. Giving way to even the likes of Trini Lopez who kicked major ass with his latin-infused version of the collegiate standard *If I Had a Hammer.* And gave future rays of light to the likes of Carlos Santana and the masterful East L.A. band Los Lobos.

Eleanor Rigby, by John Lennon and Paul McCartney. Mid-sixties pop music meets Thomas Hardy novel-like storyline and features cello and lyrics about the loneliness, tedium, boredom and death without fanfare, almost unnamed. A universe away from car-accident songs like *Teen Angel* and *Leader of the Pack* from earlier in the decade, where death was celebrated as a form of dedication and true love. That is, you pledged your eternal heart to the boy or girl who died in the car crash. I think the Everly Brothers actually did one about a plane crash.

American Pie, by New Rochelle, New York's Don McLean. Not since Bob Dylan's 1965 *Like A Rolling Stone* had a song longer than two and a half minutes get substantial and continual airplay on U.S. radio. The last line about "The Father, Son and The Holy Ghost, they caught the last train for the coast, the day the music died ..." rides in the imagination to this day though the song was released in 1971. The reverberation of those lines lamenting the traditional values of faith and American wholesomeness have been revisited by country star Garth Brooks in an *Up With People*-type rendering. And by Madonna, albeit a few lines as opposed to the full nine minute version, giving McLean the biggest royalty cheque of his career.

I Get Around, by Brian Wilson and The Beach Boys. Unlike the heady *Good Vibrations* that suggested Wilson was into psychedelia, this teenage surf/car tune comes out of the gates full throttle and displays brilliant harmony and joy of sun and water. Though it celebrates, in nuance, teenage male infidelity ("None of the guys go steady 'cause it wouldn't be right to leave your best girl home on a Saturday night"), the verve of seeking happiness makes it hard not to play the song at least twice in a row and get in your jalopy and go visit Frank and Joe Hardy (The Hardy Boys) in fictional Bayport.

A Whiter Shade of Pale, by Keith Reid for Procol Harum (in Latin *Beyond these things*). In this Bach meets Chaucer's *Canterbury Tales*, Reid got Harum onto the charts with surrealism and non-sequitur narrative. Though the song was played to death after the attempt-to-be-hip movie, *The Big Chill*, its lyricism sustains itself regardless of the tiring antic-driven acting of Kevin Kline and his prep-boy, man-stays-young Pat Boone-ishness. As did many of the great British bands of the time, Procol Harum distinctly drew references from literature as opposed to the world of television and other media. Though the song carries a *semiotic* to it, it is not a message as much as an aura of magnificence of imagination and the mind that holds the song forever high in the line-up of tunes exposed by American radio.

I Don't Like Mondays, by Bob Geldof and The Boomtown Rats. The British (Irish) returned after half a decade of Bruce Springsteen and singer-songwriters like James Taylor, Jim Croce and John Denver. Geldof and the producers of the video (as the 80s were the height of video) set his ragged harlequin looks against a backdrop of British middle class-ness with the parents and the band sitting, watching the telly, as news of a girl shooting up a classroom in San Diego came to light in the British media. This song, with its courage to expose the underbelly of a young girl's madness and dissatisfaction is the counter-balance to the lyrical *She's Leaving Home* by The Beatles in the summer of '67. When the girl was asked by the authorities why she shot her fellow students, she replied: *I don't like Mondays!* The clip, punk-infused, popism of Geldof and his band captures the edgy sentiment of unhappiness with Thatcherism and boredom of being. Video brought us many great visuals for the songs they interpreted and as far as the form was new, the inventiveness was high as new mediums always have a vanguard of artists who break as much ground as possible in their explorations of social and political conditions.

Fast Car, by Tracy Chapman. For all The Beach Boys and Bruce Springsteen car songs, this 1980s Grammy winner in the Best Single category brought back the singer-songwriter at her/his best acoustic aura. In the language of "symbol" and "semiotics," Chapman, as an African-American, signified the disenfranchised, inner city black youth that was economically challenged and dreamed of escape. The desire to get in a "fast car" and drive away from the trap of poverty varies greatly from the Beach Boy fun driving and Springsteen's teenage and young man romantic need to get away from the suffering of the city and "nowhereness." In reference to males, the car is an obvious metaphor for sexuality. But Chapman's narrator is a gentle, hurt woman who wants just a bit of relief if not the total dream of escape. There is a feel to the song that suggests: *Even if I could do it only once in a while, things might be better.* Chapman's *Fast Car* is without growls (as in Springsteen) and not merely a moaning for the road. It is a plea. The song's release was a decisive moment for the return of the acoustic, singer-songwriter as American radio came out of Punk and was on the cusp of Grunge and Rap, though teen male Metal never feared for a loss of audience.

Fight the Power, by Chuck D. and Public Enemy. The articulation of rage and the return of long language songs with political force and intent. In the tradition of Langston Hughes and the feel of The Black Panthers, Public Enemy took the title from an old James Cagney movie and turned the Irish on its head. Cursing and challenging the icons of white culture (Elvis and John Wayne), Public Enemy also introduced "Rap" to a mass audience and its true uninterrupted "Blackness." It was: *Move over white culture time. Listen to the voices of rage in your impoverished inner cities!* And: *We don't need you!* attitude. With Public Enemy, other bands such as NWA (Niggers With Attitude) and the film-making of Spike Lee, African-Americans found their way onto the airwaves without the glitter of Berry Gordy's Motown and the soft romantic sounds of Marvin Gaye and the Supremes. It was also the flip-side to Michael Jackson's Neverland fantasies and Vegas-propelled expression of African-American experience and paved the way for Hip Hop, Gangsta Rap and even the anomaly of the white and angular Eminem into the two-thousand decade.

Hurt, by Trent Reznor and Nine Inch Nails. The band's name alone gives you the depth of the narrator's Jesus-on-the-Cross suffering, though many would argue that Christ never suffered self-indulgence and Freudian whining. This song experienced a second tiering when the ailing C&W, man-in-black icon Johnny Cash was filmed at a piano with aging and quivering fingers and a face full of doubt and humility, singing: *You can take it all, my empire of dirt. I will let you down. I will make you hurt.* Both an atheistic and Christian interpretation of the lyric can't avoid the mature expression of pain. And reckoning of the human soul against its own evils with the articulation of what Jean-Paul Sartre and the French existentialists referred to "as living without deliverance and the hope for it as you wake up to your next day."

THE INTERNET CAFÉ

Espresso is espresso and an internet connection is a world of light, with rays and waves to the satellites that allow their function, crowding the invisible yet increasing weight of ether.

Some cafés acquiesce to the gods of Bill and Steve with plug-in stations throughout while organic coffee brews for at least a quarter or more than the traditional pricing at Italian cafés. You won't find old men in rumpled sports coats playing cards and smoking endless cigarettes at the modern internet café. They, in their age, have been left to their wives and shopping for rapini and tending their gardens against the harshness of northern climes. Instead, the internet café spectrums from soccer mom yoga mat carriers to young men with scruffy half-beards and The Gap's latest bad plaid Bermuda shorts. Rocking their babies back and forth through simulated '70s aviator sunglasses and a big dog (always a big dog) to catch the fancy of most of the other patrons also with a big dog (or sometimes a small dog treated like a big dog).

And it's not hard to imagine as the world turns more surreal, a day when all the yoga mats and aviator sunglasses and babies are gone and grown and the dogs (big dogs) sit and caffeine their brains out to the tune of *Sultans of Swing* and say under their breath: *I thought they would never leave!* —while howling with barky laughter and panting for water. (Seems the only reason for the dog owners to change the iPod setting and put in or take out their earplugs). Needless to say, there will be no tipping, but maybe a wag of a tail. —WOOF! WOOF! And in semiotic wonder (see Roland Barthes reference in a later section) there will be a city ordinance that all stop and go traffic signals will require barks of various types and lengths before crossing the street in a new Rover's Babylon.

GERRY "THE FAIRY" AND THE JABOUR BROTHERS

In my old hometown before I claimed another town as home, there was a granite and limestone ridge elevated over paved streets, running down to a river. There were many of those ridges with the layered rock suggesting a primordial Time. A time of cavemen and women as modernity tried to rise to the occasion of time and space. As these ridges were elevated, they usually had a sloped and flat green back with shrub and forest growth. Often a street person could be found sleeping on a cardboard box from the nearest department store. Or a mattress thrown away by one of the many growing working-class families in the area. Because the height and exposed limestone layering hung over the street below, the back end (where we ran and played and killed snakes) was named Nanny Goat Hill (implying what it took to negotiate the Hill's rock and craggy stubble).

One day as I chased my brother down The Hill with great enthusiasm and vigour, a man in a trench coat and cap (he looked like he might have been from a wharf in Hamburg) leapt up from his sleep. He stood there with nothing on under his trench coat but a pair of boxer shorts and long black knee socks. My brother yelled "Run!" as the man hollered at our trespass and his eyes winched under a set of eyebrows that seemed made of steel wool. "It's Gerry the Fairy!"

As we made it to the street and the smell of oven bread from a nearby house, we caught our breath. My brother went on to tell me that "Gerry the Fairy" was known in the neighbourhood for flashing both boys and girls and the occasional housewife. "Should we tell Dad?" I asked. "He already knows," my brother responded. "Why do you call him a *fairy*? Isn't a fairy a girl, like Tinkerbell, small and blonde and pretty?" "They call him a fairy because he doesn't have a wife and scares little kids."

As I look back to those years of childhood and brotherly camaraderie, I recall the skill at wordplay both my brother and I had inherited from our mother who could sing and rhyme like a nightingale when she wasn't chasing us down with a switch or spraying us with a water hose to beat the inner city lower town heat in summer. And I think of how that name has embedded itself in my memory. *Fairy*. Not because of the suggestion of his perversion but because of the rhyme of the nomenclature itself and how it covered the sadness, loneliness, desperation and slight mental imbalance that was likely this old man's circumstance.

By his nickname and look, Gerry became a "myth" to us. One of sleaze and unkempt-ness and warped sensibility. The "signage" we assigned him was no less cruel than scientists putting electrodes on research monkeys and then claiming it disturbed their (the monkeys') sleep. Though not totally responsible for the denigration of another human being's character (he was thus named long before we came along), our sense of secular catholicism allowed us to put food out for him when he wasn't around or was asleep on his cardboard—even if just to see him come out for it. The last time I saw Gerry I was alone. He was walking up to the top of The Hill to the cliff side, 30-feet up over the street. I remember how gently the wind tried to iron out the wrinkles of his long light-brown trench coat, and how strongly it held him as he stood at the cliff's edge, looking down.

• • •

"Goddam Jabour Brothers!" Carson would say on his way back from the grocery-hardware store where he was employed as a delivery/stock boy. Carson was old enough to have a steady job. French-Irish in ancestry, he stood low to the ground with slicked back duck-tailed hair, while shuffling in his Wellington boots with jean cuffs turned up a la Teddy-boy-Greaser. Carson was semi-literate. Couldn't really read through a comic book. But he was older (even than my brother) by a good five years so we tended to take his word as authoritative. "Goddam cheap Jabour Brothers!" he would stammer though with pride that he had work.

The Jabour Brothers were actually three brothers from Lebanon who had emigrated to North America to try and make it in the "Dream." Short on humour, they worked long days and nights to keep up an inventory for the French, Italian, Lebanese, Irish mix of immigrants raising families and themselves chasing the Dream. They were Maronite Christians and you could see them in suits on Sundays. But Carson never expressed resentment for their "otherness"—only for the long demanding hours his employment with them required.

And with this, I remember the one African-American gentleman who would come to my mother's house on bread-making day and knock on the door as he removed his hat. And that my mother brought out a loaf and placed it in his hands (open like Jesus multiplying fish yet without stigmata) and he would nod his thanks slowly and surely until next week. And through my mother's actions, our eyes would look at this man of height and his great silent dignity and emotionally would take on his cool and gentility into the day.

FAILING ART CLASS
AND BUILDING A MODEL
FROM SCRATCH
(MAKE THAT SCOTCH!)
IN THE KEY OF F

"Our assignment for next week is for you to hand in an Eskimo soap-carving," Mrs. Andrews announced in late spring grade nine. We were to buy a bar of Ivory soap and look at the pictures of Inuit art and freely copy a style from one of her art book texts. I hated Ivory soap given a skin condition I had as a kid. It left my skin dry and itchy and the smell was nauseous to my system. Weeks earlier I had handed in a peculiar imitation of Van Gogh swirling clouds with purples and yellows and a Mexican bandit standing with guns ready by a desert cactus. I still don't know where that came from. Maybe from seeing *The Magnificent Seven* with Eli Wallach piercing threats into Yul Brynner's Russian-accented gun-slinger. But I got an A for it and thought I could cruise my way through the soap-carving assignment.

So when it came time to hand in the carving and Mrs. Andrews awed and wowed at the work that other students were handing in, I told her I had forgotten my bar of soap on the bus to school. Not good enough was the verdict. My zero on that negated the A and I came up with an F. Next up was grade ten and a photo essay of some kind.

Having an older brother who was good with cameras and ship and car models, it dawned on me that I could take his racing car models (that had working engines in them), grab his camera and shoot the cars as they raced around a figure eight track. There I was, all set to shoot. Hitting the release button as the cars flew around, and trying to hold a camera in the other hand and catching stills of the cars as they raced around. I was totally excited at the prospect of amazing shots coming out. "No one is gonna have any photo essay like this!" I thought, as the pasta cooked in the kitchen and my brother tuned a guitar in his room next to me. "Okay, I'm coming," I said, answering my mother's call to the dinner table. And assured myself: "I'll get this finished after dinner."

Dinner was superb but, as I sat there into my tenth meatball, I couldn't think of anything but cars flying down the track and the smile that would bring to my teacher's face. Dinner having ended and the family hunkered down to some prime time TV, I sat on the floor of my bedroom cross-legged and fumbled around with the camera and cars. Ten shots in I thought I had enough footage to make a great sequence. The next evening I took the film roll in for developing and thought cars, cars, cars for a week. When they came in, they were blurred yet colourful. Kind of like one of those Einstein descriptions of what happens to stationary bodies when they move through time. But you couldn't make out the cars' shape unless you were told. My stomach clenched as the photo essay had to be handed in the next morning.

"What happened?" my brother asked. "Did you get an A?" "No." An extension. An A for effort but an F for presentation. What to do? An extension usually meant you got another shot at a project or at least more time. In this case I had two days. There was no way my brother or I could figure out the magic of catching the cars in motion 'cause we didn't have any kind of movie camera. So one night as my brother was out folk-singing his heart out, I snuck into his room, grabbed some airplane glue and a little box model of a Spitfire and sat myself down cross-legged on the floor again. My idea was to take a couple of shots of a finished model I would put together myself and present it to the teacher.

Dinner time came 'round again and, given it was close to Christmas, my dad had his friend drop in afterwards and they raised a glass of wine, then a glass of scotch. As I was asked to clean off the table after my dad and his pal's ribaldry, and being in the kitchen alone, I took the drink glasses and noticed some remains that looked sorta like ginger-ale. The taste was deep and hard. I gasped for water and, taking a sip, I felt kind of good but a bit dizzy. I returned to my position on my bedroom floor and resumed the model building. "How do I get this glue out of this little tube?" I asked myself. The model had so many pieces. "How does he do it?" I asked, trying to channel my brother's finger dexterity.

I managed to snap the end of the tube off with my teeth and noticed the smell was sweet but I had to get the glue out of my mouth. I couldn't figure out how you could stick the pieces of the model together from such a small tube, still I hung in, rubbing at my nose in the process. I felt dry in the mouth and thought that ginger-ale drink in the kitchen was good. I snuck the bottle out of the cupboard my dad kept his 'goods' in and took another sip. I tip-toed to my model as I could hear the TV on in the rec room downstairs. My room smelled like glue as my fingers pulled and pushed the model into shape. I sneezed twice and my throat went numb.

Next morning I took my model into class. "The wings are backwards," my teacher informed me. "Where is the photograph?" "Well, there's one on the model box. See," I said, holding up the image of the Spitfire. "Yes but you were supposed to take a picture, no?" "The camera didn't work 'cause it got glue stuck on it," I offered. "Well, you're going to have to have an F for this," my teacher announced for all to hear. More disappointed than embarrassed, I moped at my desk and thought: "At least it's getting close to Christmas. Maybe I will have some more of that ginger-ale for the holidays. Maybe I should try playing my brother's guitar." It took me years to learn how to tune it. A sip of scotch always brings that laborious process up a notch. Thank God for automatic tuners. In the key of F — all is forgiven.

VANCOUVER PINES

Height. That's the eye's first experience as I wander this Pacific city with its shorelines and rolling streets. Then the myth of one being at the end of the continent (but for Alaska above you) and the feeling of lumberjacks and whales and islands that can take you even further away. But there's little relief from your sense of wonder which becomes an entrapment of sorts. An entrapment bound by sea on one side and mountains on the other. The immediate feeling is at once a sense of freedom and being stuck. Together these two sensations run with you and you find the salmon inevitably fantastic yet the bears a bit too plentiful—especially when you wander off the well-trodden paths by mountain golf courses—and then as they say—you are really "in the woods."

Black bear! Ah oooh! At least it's not a wolf or a grizzly chasing you up a tree. You got a chance to escape and leave Big Smokey to all the salmon berries and mud he wants. Of course, he can be a she and that's even more dangerous. You'd feel like a major moron if you came across a mother who wanted space for her young. You know, intruding without any indication you had planned a visit. Didn't call ahead. You learn respect fast unless you're an idiot. You don't even have to be ecologically-minded. Just scared out of your pants. If you're lucky you find your well-hooked ball and scurry out. If you're not, you're walking mud-trails back to the greenhouse with your pants full of burrs and your head full of growls and teeth.

Then of course there is the placid approach. There you are on the sixth hole ready to tee off and in the distance a black bear and her cubs walk leisurely across the fairway and you and your day partners wonder at the loping ease with which the mother bear leads her young across this man-made acreage. But at least here you can see the furry enemy. Not like playing a filled-in-swamp outside of West Palm Springs, Florida when you thought your ball was going to land smack on the green and it ends up by a mini-lake, just on the edge of the water trap. So you think: *Maybe I'll retrieve that one. I'm down to three so I better, otherwise I'm gonna have to borrow another and go through the ritual of* You lost another — ha ha! *ribaldry known to many a once-in-a-blue-moon golfer.*

There you go. Towards the edge of the water and in the middle of the water pool you see bubbles and your drunken partners make jokes about your ball drowning. And of course you've walked far ahead to get that ball and avoid the embarrassment and, just as you put your hand in to troll with your fingertips, you hear a snap and gurgle and it's nothing less than an alligator looking for lunch. Of course, the warning from your partners comes much too late and there you are with wet shoes and only two balls left in your bag. "Ha ha ha!" the merriment goes and between the bears and alligators you know you aren't in Disneyland 'cause these things don't smile and shake your hand with big friendly paws and dopey head nods.

And you think: *What kind of karma is in this? Almost getting mauled by a black bear or losing a middle finger to a gator?* Karma like the woman on the sea bus talking hippie and new age all at once and the likelihood that you would have asked her out to a movie if she didn't keep going on about the karmic truths of each human movement. All this to say—You could die on a beach or in the woods out in the great North woods and nobody would hear about it. And that's the long loneliness of the high pines with their constant coniferous reach to the sky regardless of the incessant rain.

This ain't East and the cityscape of bustling downtown neighbourhoods. This is volcano and monsoon and earthquake/mudslide country! And they carved a city out of it! And somewhere some real karma may come down and it feels like it could be any time soon. High pines. Vancouver pines. The word *pine* itself. The mourning of it. The troubled drug-infested city square off Gastown where non-archetypical junkies sit on street-corners and don't even ask you for a dollar. This is the down low part. The part the city doesn't invite you to. The magazines on the airplanes and *The National Geographic* good looking lady scientist rock-climbing yet another peak while her kids go kayaking with lawyer dad and the perfection of teeth.

This is the hell the city fathers and mothers don't want you to see. You are better off eaten by a bear than being accosted by a street junkie who has lost her card-boarded flat and hasn't seen a relative since her parents put her up for adoption thirty years ago in some mid-western plains town with apples on the trees and flocks of crows cawing the sky. This is where the height "comes down" and the Jesus the lady on the sea bus talks about to whom all sing praises on more than only Sundays. This is the awful height of paradise. West and East of Eden at the same time. Alligators, pines and bears aside.

THE DEATH OF *SENSU* (SEXUALITY)

Yoga and you ain't just meditating as your latest date says: "Do you believe in Tantric sexuality?" You answer that you haven't had a fit for a long time and there goes language again! "No, not since I was nine and my brother threw an orange at my head!" "Oh, that's awful. Did it hurt?" "No, he missed but he broke the window when I ducked." And so begins the reduction of sexual impulse to psycho-sexual conversation thus the donuts and the pizza will have to wait.

What is it that our western culture desires from infusing and inhaling traditional oriental and Asian meditative traditions including ones that take sexual impulses and reduce them to ether? Buddhism, neo-tantra and lattes all mix together to cut the lines and angles of modernization and attempt to effect the blood-brain barrier in a transcendent manner. Sitting aside all this is a verve for body and the "pornographic" yet the term "pornographic" seems to suggest a "voyeurism" more than a sexual practice, given its availability through our internet technology following publication upon publication of the hustle and tumble magazines of earlier decades.

The culture we live in seems to suggest that it is wonderful to have a website dedicated to the creation of cup-cakes and wholesomeness while our sons and daughters attend bars and clubs late into the weekend dressed to kill and manifest the olfactory wonders of perfume and cologne variations.

So when your date wants to tell you about Tantric sex and the practices of ego-less body pleasure, the hypocrisy increases as you lie on your bed and wonder what it just might have been like to engage in the actual act of love-making. And if you offer, in the midst of one of these pre-love-making situations, the classical Greek myth of Orpheus and Eurydice, you might find that culture skipped a hurdle in the long run to pleasure, knowledge and even spirituality.

So what should we get on the pizza?
I don't eat pizza or panini or any gluten.
You don't have to eat a lot of it.
No. I mean gluten. My mother is a naturopath.
Has she seen a doctor?
She doesn't need to.
Chinese?
Have you heard what the Republican Chinese are doing re: the Dali Lama?
You mean the bald guy who laughs all the time?
I feel like a latte.
I know this Italian place around the corner . . .

I will not have Fascist espresso!

Cuban?

Oh, we had a Salsa class the other night and it was packed. I brought my sneakers for the class and then changed into my heels to dance at the club later.

Did you eat?

Martinis. Martinis. Martinis.

That's an Italian drink, isn't it?

No. American.

You American?

No but we were brought up Christian Fundamentalists.

And so there you are with no prospects for food and on the verge of more ego-driven conversation and maybe all because you could have spared yourselves the time and coffee expense and just approached it all by internet dating. But in this culture of have-and-get-it-all we all seem to need space. Not outer but inner space. (Well, come to think of it, both.)

Robert Frost in his poem *The Star Splitter* has his main character say: *the best thing that we're put here's for's to see* . . . Yet the failed farmer of his poem decides to watch stars at night and burn down his barn so he can collect the insurance money and buy a telescope. An exact realization of the connection between "inner" and "outer" space. A desire to be part of a myth or be witness to it. A cut right through the contemporary new age psychology. A pragmatic approach to living in the moment and the sensuality of the soul without the semantic babble and protracted delay of experience which takes even our sexuality down a step.

Not that we are dying to rut and tumble, but that we are denying the feeding of our spiritual core by 3D-ing and "screening" our world before we jump into it. Supposedly, the mind is still quicker than the fastest computer. The mind's speed including the ability to imagine and recollect and envision a future without the aid of others' or mechanical interpretation. *There is too much light and not enough "hum."* Too much tantric and not enough love and exploration. Too many ideas and no execution. Yet there are suggestions of renaissance when 100 guitar players (who are not professional—nor are they good) sit in a park on Sunday and pursue fame within their small group. Though most will not crack the code of mythology (being something bigger than you are), they at least have entered the stewing-pot of the fickle codes of dandyism and poseur-ism. Scratchy beards and bad clothes-matching and personal aesthetics aside.

There is always room for conversation. Talk to any old Italian man or woman. Never read a book or sat at a computer screen. For that matter, forget they are Italian and learn the power of their illiteracy. The ability to intuit and feel and make sense of a "humming" world. As for *sensu*(sexuality)—small wonder they had so many kids.

INTERNET DATING PROFILES,
OR: *DO YOU LIKE DOGS AND SEMIOTICS?*

Janie's Profile:

Well, what can I say about myself? I have a dog. Nice dog. Hasn't bitten anyone for, oh, let's say ... about five years. But that was not her fault. There was this guy who wasn't happy that I was going to move to the Northwest Territories and one day he came over and began to pack his things and in the process picked up by accident my dog's playball. The dog started barking but he was into his own rage and head so much that he didn't realize he'd taken the dog toy. Well, as he was taking the boxes out to his van, Dog-girl ripped into his right leg and he dropped the box. Then of course he blamed me for the fractured toe he received from the falling box.

I teach. I play piano and like gardening. I'm about five foot seven and sometimes go out winter camping. I love summer though because it's time off from the constant day-in, day-out work-work of teaching special needs. I have special needs too and maybe if you like what you read you can help with them? My last good thought was when someone asked me what my last good thought was. I was surprised that I was asked and it took me back to another time and place as I was in the immediate moment of response.

I don't think women like guys to be complicated. Most women want guys to be nice, secure, interesting and positive and tender, loving and a go-out-and-get-it type of man. I don't see a contradiction in that but it must be complicated being a guy? That said: you can't live with them and you can't live without them. That's why I'm writing this.

Is there anyone out there who isn't going to talk about sports and classic rock? Knows jazz and likes to walk with me and my Dog-girl? Has a great car? Doesn't want a clinging girl? (Though last time I cleaned the house there were a lot of clinging dog hairs).

I'm off for two months during summer. I would love to see Europe and other parts of the world. A fellow teacher (a speech pathologist) told me he really liked traveling, especially to the Mediterranean countries because people use their hands when they talk and I'm pretty well-trained in ASL.

My favourite place to go is the gardens down by the lakefront. I like a guy with strong hands. Some of my friends wish I would answer my phone more often. I like communication. I don't necessarily look at the stars at night and can't name more than one or two constellations and even that is only because I think it has something to do with astrological signs which I read everyday.

If you think I'm interesting and not complicated I would be happy to meet for a coffee (make that mint tea). I don't think they should charge the same for mint tea as they do for coffee. What do you think? Oh yes, and there's more about me!!!

The reason I don't like phones is that I suffered having to work day in day out doing telemarketing—yecch bigtime! Sooo, if I don't call you back or if I invite you to a barbeque it might take forever and a long time. Please don't ask me what barbeques have to do with phones.

I do like sending emails once in a while. There is this guy I 'kinda' like and I invited him for a bbq but my bbq has broken down. You might think I'm weird that I haven't invited him for dinner in the meantime. Thing is, I like to be mysterious but other people think I'm rude but I think I'm right. You might ask, 'Right about what?' and that, I must admit is a pretty good question.

I'm also into practicing piano and conflict resolution. One of the ways I practice the latter is by withdrawing like a turtle. I think that's a great amphifan or animal (not sure which) but I like it 'cause it's got a long neck like me. You might ask— 'Doesn't it hurt carrying a shell around all day and stretching my neck into the water or digging a hole to hide my head in the earth?' That too is a good question. You seem to ask all the right questions and say all the right things. You sure you don't know me better than I know myself or are you just highly perceptive? Geez, it's hard to be mysterious when someone is perceptive and complicated to boot!

Anyway, back to this guy. He seems to like me but is not impressed with my manner. He bought me a piano lesson but not a piano. I have one already and my dog likes it when I play 'most' of the time.

I also have to get home at midnight because my pumpkin-red hair will turn green if I don't. That's hard to explain but I think that's why Cinderella was traveling in a carriage because if her head turned green no one would see it. It would sure help if this guy had a car. Then my head could turn green in his face and I wouldn't have to run home by subway though if it were St. Patrick's Day I guess it would be okay. How's that for mystery?!

What else to say about myself and what I want? Well, the last guy I was with was a meanie. He said bad things and wouldn't move to the NWT even though they have great potatoes and starlight. I have a friend who's seeing a guy from the Middle East or somewhere hot. He's a meanie too! Goes out with my best friend. I guess me and my best friend talk about meanies when she doesn't get embarrassed that she is with one. He and I don't get along to say the least.

I know I'm going on but I want you to know as much as possible before we meet. If we meet?

I was hurt before but I'm gaining my courage back. I hope you're the right guy. Remember that I've learned a lot from conflict resolution. It's what special needs teachers do. Oh, did I forget to tell you that? That's my job. But it's summer now and I am going to try to get my head out of the sand just enough to see who's out there in the world of interesting and unattached men.

Oh, another note. I like tall handsome men. I don't really like anglo guys with grey hair though it makes a difference if there's a car there somewhere. So if you are that guy, I am the gal!!!

And another thing. Just because I don't show interest doesn't mean I'm not interested.

Understand?

I would attach a photo with this but I am spending most of the summer with my new wrap-around sunglasses on disguised as Spiderman's Sister. I know ... I know ... you're thinking: "Wow — what mystery and Holy Halloween all summer long?!!"

PS

I'm also interested into semiotics and Charles Bukowski pomes.

Janie

• • •

Response to Janie's Profile:

Helloooo Janie!!!! I love dogs!!! Make that Dogs with a cap-i-t0l D! But I don't got one but would like to walk and talk about youre liking Charles

Bukooski pomes, 'cause I'm now writing my first ones. Well, okay — not really my first ones, but new ones. I went to see 'Barflyer' with Mickie O'rourke 'cause I'm irIsh too! It was free.

But I have to say I don't know what semioticks is? I'm looking for fun and think Spiderman is great! I hope you like me too . . . Let's walk!

Yours,

Patrick

pS

My sister got profile married too this year.

WORLD CUP JAZZ

nflect! Improvise! Cross the musical scale like big slow fish with long arching chord changes and harmonics —look like you listen—eyes with ears—and then run in like a bop-playing saxophonist scattering and moving sideways to the "centrifugality" of BALL!

This is jazz! This is Futbol! Set the radio mid-volume and turn the TV announcers down. Put the phone on vibrate and bring up Coltrane as the Argentine side shimmies an attack up-field against the forever England Team. Ain't no one saying anything as your ears jump and sally, ride and perch, whistle and turn. Inflect! Improvise! Release at the exact moment of least resistance. It's a long play. Play making can last minutes on end and the ref can change that but commercials cannot. Sepp Blatter. *Giuseppe* with a last name that sounds like a body organ. PLAY THE BALL! The head of Zidane! (Strange?) — The head of Pele. (Crown of Laurels) — The head of Maradona. (Banditry) *Bring me the head of Alfredo Garcia!* to borrow a phrase from the ever-so violent Sam Peckinpah 1974 film.

So goes the memory of the World Cup in 1998 — a year after my mother died (too early). American football didn't seem to make as much sense with its rough ten second plays and whistles and commercials and predictability and rock & roll. *Too much **NOISE!*** I thought as I lay sleepless for a good few months, having seen my own ghost a few nights before the final. What is it about American Football that makes it adolescent, testosterone-driven and hard-edged compared to World Cup Soccer? Perhaps my own state of having lost the eternal/maternal safety of womb had something to do with the perception at the time?

I know as I watched the Italians, French, Brazilians et al come together over a soccer field, there was a way to do it without listening to the drivel and drive of announcers that both sports have in common. The "GOL! GOL! GOL! GOL! GOLGOL — GOL! GOL! GOOOOLLL! OOOOOOLLLLLLL!" of Latin-American announcers rivals the best of John Madden/Al Michaels hunkaburnin' love NASCAR oratory. But the sport(s)? Different as night and day! Different as Springsteen and Queen cheer-leading frolics from Miles Davis and Dizzy Gillespie lateral ascending-descending scales and harmonics *sans* vocals. *(Nota bene: It is important that there be no vocals for the jazz chosen to accompany World Cup Futbol.)*

Spanish side like light rain against the goonish Netherlands? This was 2010, the Final and the horns that sounded like a thousand bees drove the early morning North American audiences nuts! But Spain with its exactness, grace and precision managed to overcome the height and elbows of a once proud Total Football nation. The one of Johan Cruyff and Neeskens and Bergkamp. What did it mean to have such reversal? The new Asian and African teams with their speed and agility? It meant more jazz! Higher pitched and wheeling! Great thrusts forward but never alone. Each set of feet seeing the feet on the other side of the field.

It was not push and pull and stammer on your heels waiting for the referee to throw a flag and prolong the last two minutes of a game as though there was everything left on earth to sell. From insurance, to medicine (with suicide tendency caveats) to cars (really big monster trucks) to a once in a while good society exposé on the latest 'big guy' doing good things for the hard-hit communities. But this can't be done without stopping the game. Making the game last almost three and a half hours. A game that in truth is only played on the field for sixty minutes.

Days before the two-thousand-ten final my father passed away. His favourite pieces of music were Southern Italian tarantellas. He didn't know Coltrane but dug James Taylor. It wasn't jazz but he believed, when I showed him a photo of big Charlie Bird, that he would have been a great goal-tender. I put on Hugh Masekela, turned down the volume of the television again and watched the light of nimble and fashionable feet in highlight reruns, thinking what kind of music would work with cricket?

FATHER, IT'S TIME—
IS IT PIAZZA OR PIZZA ITALYUN?

You ever been Italian? Ever been part Italian or first or second or third generation Italian? Sicilian or Calabrese or Neapolitan? Venetians and Milanese (with apologies) don't count in this. *Sopranos* fans do. *Godfather* fans as well. Still, historical and cultural figure do. Even talk of Fermi and Dante, Fellini and Madonna and Big Frank. And mostly sons and daughters, wives and grand kids that came with the migration over the course of the last half century. "Delissio" Time! "East Side Mario's." Capone. Scorsese. Coppola and Ferlinghetti. And if you didn't know and if you don't care to—Steven Segal! Steve Tyler! And—and—and even Bruce Springsteen and Jon Bon Jovi!

So this is the gig. You're invited to perform on one of the city's biggest stages and it's all to celebrate "Festa della Repubblica"

(Italy's national holiday—June 2—and 2010 marks the 150th. Coincidentally the start of the American Civil War). So there you are amidst the inheritors of the immigrant experience and you're a singer and musician to boot! And you wrote a song that won a prestigious award and addressed the history of family and migration and the movement to another shore. And though the sociology seems to suggest your progenitors' story is more relevant than your own—you get *your story* in there "*... Father, it's time. Time we should talk. By evening the moon disappears.*" And it rings a bell for *woppos* (a bastardization of the Spanish *guapo* (good-looking) and *wop* (**W**ith **O**ut **P**apers) and critics alike. But they decide to call the event "Piazza Italia" which means "Italian Square" but really hope it to mean "where people gather." Though the word visually is strikingly similar to the word pizza, which everyone knows is round and can be as deep-dish as Al Capone liked it.

You ever want to be Italian? Where the food means everyone is happy—having roll on roll of bun and laughter, prosciutto and lasagna—sing a pepperoni song and twilight to Sinatra and Tony Bennett? Pose with loads of siblings and extended family? This is what *Pizza* Italia wants. The question is—is this what *Piazza* Italia, and its proponents, inevitably desire as well? And what is it sons and daughters of those who travelled hard from agrarian shores want? The doctors, actors, writers, lawyers, politicians, etc.? "That's not Italian, not even *I-tal-yun!*," one says trying to muster up all the New Jersey wise-guy attitude he can get his vocal chords on, as he gnaws into some deep Chicago-style crust.

What does it all mean? To call something Piazza Italia? What's wrong or right with the signs (semiotics), the representation? A pizza is a pizza. An espresso an espresso. Italian nationalism it is not. You can't pretend a north American busy downtown square is Piazza Navona in Rome. You can only pretend it is a North American downtown square and grasp hopelessly for the myth if you are so disposed. And your father might tell you: *I used to sing for a bite to eat. Sing from town to town in my part of Italy.* And you can't argue with him that he did or didn't. And you maybe think to yourself : *I ain't that hungry but I got to put the song out anyway. Regardless of the phantasmagoria of Garibaldi/Michelangelo and all the "oiliness" of the Medicis and Borgias, that somehow crosses the Atlantic in tuna and sardine tins and ends up on your deep-sixer Pi(a)zza.*

ROLAND BARTHES AND TODD GITLIN

(The Interpretation of Meaning and Media)

All of language is a constellation of SIGNS. All the MEDIUMS through which language and its signs are delivered ARE NOT LANGUAGE. If you disagree, or are a mailman who has just about had it with the dogs on his route—you can be first in line to declare your objections to this premise.

What is interpretation but making the "subject at hand" your own? In Nicholas Roeg's 1970s film *Insignificance* an archetypal Marilyn Monroe explains the Special Theory of Relativity to an archetypal Albert Einstein. She uses trains and balloons and flashlights while he is haplessly transfixed by her breasts and lips and nods his head in agreement and fascination. And though Roeg is saying beauty can be intelligent (something most of us do not want to believe), the actual Theory is no more clear than it was before the scene begins.

Comforting however are the balloons. The little boy's trains. The flashlight. Her quest for elusive earth-motherhood underneath the lipstick and billowing white dress. The whole scene seems to swell with the imminent possibility of explosion. Light! Balloons! Trains! Rockets! Breasts! The universe! Neon! Male meets Female! BOOM! No wonder between the secret of the atom to the celerity of Klieg lights we need sunglasses!

• • •

BARTHES. This most intriguing mid-twentieth century French semiotician and Marxist sits with his Gauloise-stained thumb and forefinger and considers the word *apps*. How to get around this abbreviation and return to the common sense full syllables of the word *application*? For the fourteen-millionth time he is brought to his *Writing Degree Zero* (the posit that a writer must just write *without* intent political, romantic, technically or otherwise for motivation) knees. *Comment ce dit en français?* asks this man who skinned the cat on the bourgeois pretensions of a Jules Verne and underlined the tenacity of Jean Arthur Rimbaud's anti-Republicanism. "How do you say in French: *Mon dieu! Quelle merde-de-cheval? Le mot en français c'est* **application***!* Not some half-sized word made to forfeit the completeness of language, as deficient as the English tongue is! *THE MEDIUM IS NOT THE MESSAGE!*"Which remains constant in his head through his two-thousandth smoke of the week and parenthetical conjecture.

And what is the *valued* (in lay terms) *significance* of the word *apps*? Curiously it sounds like a type of snake *(asp)* if you say it *fastenough,* throw a little lisp in and you know your *ophiology*. Besides being a word that makes convenient the use of Apple computers and iPads, why do we need the abbreviation? Where is it that we need to go that shortens language like a 10-4 Call Back highway rig steaming through NASCAR country? Does it put us in touch with anything we haven't experienced or had knowledge of? Or does it simply underline our vanity and ultra-commercial *lemmingly-ness?*

Answer? It doesn't seem to matter what we need as much as what we want, and language in flux is a great virtue. Yet when it leads to superficiality as in achromatic signage and pretentious cool-hip cliquishness, problems can develop in substance and cleverness as knowledge becomes isolated packs of syllables, and to some detriment, is imitated orally. Thus, the signage of *app* might be considered against the signage of $\mathbf{E} = \mathbf{MC^2}$. Most people are learning what an *app* is. Many assume to know what Einstein was saying. The former is a sign of little existential value wherein the latter relates the core to our understanding of the physical universe within and beyond our planet. Yet perhaps a function of an *app* could be to point you to a detailed reading of The Special Theory of Relativity.

The "danger" of course is that one reads the abbreviated version and ingests a generality re: the Theory and this can be related to any subject matter from *Moby Dick* to *How to Play Chess Instructions.* And further, what holds us back from abbreviating app even further to *ap'?* — *a* followed by a *p* with an apostrophe doesn't seem to be taken *yet* in the English lexicon. Nor the computer-jargoned mindset? How does *app* win out? One might argue that it is a logical sequence to abbreviate the word.

Question: Why didn't it exist before it appeared? It certainly wasn't a street urchin who came up with the term and then it ascended the social ladder. In fact, it began at the top of the economic chain — i.e. corporations — and has *infiltrated* downwards much like the first television sets which were originally only affordable by the wealthy and a system of want and have across all classes ensued. And beyond this *class competitiveness* is the *corporate competitiveness* that vies for our attention and often succeeds in getting our interest, and sometimes even our sympathy. Not unlike the way in which we become aficionados of a certain type of coffee. Or espresso machine. Or hockey stick. Or sports team.

We follow the label and in turn are labelled. *No?* Look at your latest apple or tomato or t-shirt or subway steps. **Stickers — logos everywhere and ne'er a chance to think!** I heard of a elderly woman who tripped and broke her hip trying to negotiate the subway stairs but couldn't find them clearly because an image of leaves and gigantic words changed the colour and tone of the steps. Visually removing the angular risers. Soon afterward, a lawyer filed suit on her behalf against the advertisers and the local transit company.

• • •

TODD GITLIN. *There is **information** and then there is **gossip**. There is **political disagreement** and then there is **rumour**.* We are all susceptible to this with at least five senses. In his fascinating exposé about identity politics and political correctness, *The Twilight of Common Dreams*, Gitlin, a professor of Media Studies at Columbia and Berkeley, writes of the fall of the 1960s and early '70s New Left. A later text (*Media Unlimited*) is dedicated to the study of media, in which he underscores the speed with which mass media has now situated itself as the heartbeat of contemporary western society. Gitlin studies the incremental increase in the ascension of images. From pre-historic cave drawings and the first European paintings to the imposition on rural, small-town culture by neon and the rapid transformation from electric (radio and TV and film) to the electronic (internet). He argues that the increase in external "signage," particularly the *speed*, challenges the ability to not overcrowd the brain and allow the development and subtlety of *critical thinking*.

From Gitlin we get a sense that the information highway is loaded with waste product that takes on meaning simply because it exists and diverts attention from the substance of communication. A question to pose here after Gitlin's consideration is: If the medium is argued to be the message, as McLuhan said, *what is the message in the medium?* One message is *attainment.* Another is attainment of *power.* Another is flooding and saturation. Another yet is loss of individuality and identity or the fight and struggle for it. And further, the making of new or hidden identity. Yet all this can not be done without the utilization and recognition of *signs* — *micro,* as in the compaction of internet sites and information, and *macro,* as in massive billboards on the sides of buildings in almost all modern downtown cities.

In studying the nature of political correctness, or what Gitlin calls "identity politics," he speaks of the great divide that occurred for many in the New Left after years of focus and a determined common will to confront the established order that brought us the racism and Vietnam war in post 1950s America. He talks of how the New Left, disheartened by the rise of Reaganism, divided along colour and cultural lines. I.e.: A Chicano farmer and a draft dodger might have had a common interest in confronting laws and class oppression in an earlier decade but, as the decades advanced into the '80s and '90s, a self-centred interest took over most political and social groups. A "me first" as opposed to "we together" paradigm resulted.

The effects of this phenomenon was that an activist culture became easy prey for the divide and conquer mentality of the New Right. And with this, *signage* was used. Reagan, fatherly and folksy, became the saviour of the traditions and wholesomeness of America. Everyone else was caught trying to get in, as if coming home late and promising to cut the hedges and trim the lawn. The common dreams and aspirations of correcting the wrongs of the previous social order that brought us greed, war and hatred fell wayward. With this, the spirit of the New Left was politically decimated.

One of the most intriguing 'signs' in the '60s was Muhammad Ali, three-time heavyweight champion. African-American, a member of the Nation of Islam and a draft-dodger, Ali represented the epitome of all that resisted external order in an effort to stay true to his beliefs (identity). Even in his later years, like Einstein, Ali has taken it upon himself to be a spokesman for the down-trodden and continues his anti-war pacifist stance through the Afghan and Iraq wars.

In cultural signage this is the polar opposite to the Sylvester Stallone characters of '80s movies, who is going to get all the reds and bad guys—as either a boxer or a mercenary. He is the wild west cowboy cleaning up the globe instead of the town. He is not James Dean trying to come to terms with loveless parents or Marlon Brando's *voyous* kicking down the doors of Hollywood establishment or Paul Newman cutting off the heads of parking meters in drunken rebellion.

From Gitlin and Barthes we get an insistence to find something in ourselves: *conscience*. A sign of responsible citizenry. And media (in all forms), though tilted in favour of the advertisers and commercializers of our society and culture, is experiencing a new signage—the environmentally conscious, anti-Starbuck's youth gathering in parks and city squares. This gesture too is made of cultural signage. One that is claiming new ground and identity.

INTERVIEWING THE CRITICS

Critics, whatever vein (vain) they work in, seem to carry an authority of voice through their opinion and have been known to influence the course of an artist's career. Enhance and deepen the richness of the work they criticize or analyze or destroy what they do not concur with. Inevitably this leads to a dicey relationship between artist and critic. And the question is asked here: Who is living off whom?

Let's begin by assuming a situation that might have been part of history. And if not a part of historical fact, let's theorize a bit to expound upon the inter-relationship between critic and artist. So — i.e.: A caveman draws the sketch of an antelope he hunts so as to remember it and to possibly show to other members of his clan. Even if he is alone, he records it for a functionality. The function of recalling it. Can we assume that he has drawn this for any aesthetic purpose? That is, can aesthetic purpose be totally self-contained? That this caveman has done it for pleasure himself or for no higher purpose than merely the function of recording?

At some point along his history, the said caveman runs into another caveman and finds he is doing the same thing. Drawing with blood a sketch of an antelope. The first caveman then invites the second caveman to his cave to see his sketch and they agree it is the same animal they have both drawn. Soon the news spreads and they decide to go hunting together. They fail at finding any prey but, as the sun goes down each night, they sit and look at the drawing, either in caveman number one's or caveman number two's cave. They agree now on three things: that they both drew the same animal, that they should hunt together and that they look at their drawings together.

Later, in their hunt they hear rustling in a forest patch and the high whining sound of an animal. They run closer to the spot and see a third caveman lifting an antelope carcass onto his back and stumbling through the brush. Without fear, they run up to him. They communicate by signs and soon it is understood that they would like the third caveman to join them in either of their caves to see their drawing(s). Caveman number three, though he is carrying a heavy weight, agrees. Inside the cave, caveman number one wants caveman three to look at his drawing. Caveman three grunts and kinda laughs and jostles the weight on his shoulders but does not put it down.

Behind him caveman two is watching all this and in a jilt of jealousy at the communication between caveman one and caveman three, punches caveman three in the back and, as caveman three whirls around, caveman two picks up some dried brush and pushes caveman one aside, violently attacking the wall sketch and rubbing away most of it. Though they have no language (in the modern sense) among them, they begin to fight and argue, both gruntingly and physically. Caveman three falls to the ground with the dead antelope weight on top of him. Caveman two *now* grunts in no uncertain terms that the wall painting *is no good*. That the antelope on the ground is *really good*. Caveman one gets upset that his drawing is ruined. Thus a certain type of primitive criticism is born.

Fast forward to twenty-first century. An artist proposes to a national radio broadcaster an idea to interview critics from different fields of criticism—i.e.: music, theatre, dance, visual art, literature, multi-media *et al*. After all, what do we know about the critics around us? Where they trained? Who influenced them in their chosen fields? How they come to their decisions and authoritative voices? How did they acquire their platform to speak, offer opinion and influence?

Here Comes A Sign. In the course of the meeting, the broadcaster's representative, a little known poet, and now in charge of acquiring ideas for new programmes, *turns her eyes down*, scribbles (God knows what?) and let's the artist go on with enthusiasm, re: the possibility of the idea coming to light. **The Sign—The Eyes Going Down**. The artist can see now that she has scribbled nothing on her pad but her time for soccer-mom-ing later that afternoon. Her cell-phone rings and the meeting is cut short.

The Interview: The artist decides to hold a panel nonetheless with a music critic, a theatre critic, a dance critic and a film critic. Before the panel begins, they are all given envelopes with one image each and asked not to open them until a question is asked of them.

Artist *(to Film Critic)*: You've been writing—how long now? Can you tell us how you came to interpret the *Godfather Part 2* scene where Fredo cries out: *"I'm smaaht! I was looked over! I'm you're older brother, Mikey!"* as one of latent homosexuality?

Film Critic: Actually, the semiotic variable is a continuum from his "gayness" in *Dog Day Afternoon*.

Artist: Isn't *Dog Day* ... after *Godfather Two*?

Film Critic: Oh my god! Yes! You're right! Absolutely!! Right! Right on! Thank you!!

Artist: Getting back to the "gayness" factor? What did you mean? That Fredo loves his brother in a sort of Greek-like manner?

FC: You mean like Plato and Aristotle?

Artist: Well not really. More like a variation on Oedipus?

FC: Oh, oh!

Artist: Tell us. Where did you study criticism and who are your influences?

FC: You mean study? Where I went to College?

Artist: Yes.

FC: I was the rock critic for a regional magazine on the club scene. Mostly I liked The Doors. Some Grateful Dead. Can I open this *(referring to his envelope)* now?

Theatre Critic: Yes, why can't we open them now?

Artist: Hmm?

Dance Critic: *(Opening his ahead of time)* I don't' get it. What's this? A painting? A monstrous figure biting into a smaller body? Dance? I'm ...

Artist: Goya. *Saturn Devouring His Children*. How would you analyze it from a dance critic's perspective?

FC: Oh, come on! The semiotic language in the shape. The still movement of the symbolic eyeless monster. The sign ... the sign offers conjunction to the present-day slaughter of children throughout the world. The dance of the grotesque.

Artist: *(To film critic)* Where is it you said you studied?

FC: *(Opening his envelope)* Huh! A photograph of Al Pacino eating oysters on New York City's Mulberry Street! Fantastic!

Music Critic: *(Opening his)* Nice. Nice. A copy of the set list for the last Mötley Crüe concert!

Artist: So, I guess everything is opened?

Theatre Critic: No. Mine isn't. Should I ...?

Artist: Where did you begin your study of theatre? Can you tell me ...?

TC: I never studied anything. I used to write but didn't get any of my plays off the ground and then this critic the same day I was gonna get engaged, died. And I was asked to maybe take over the column for a while 'til a replacement came along and then—well my wife-to-be ran off with another guy ... so—I got the job—so to speak.

Artist: Who was it that died?

FC: Martin Kay. He was the Arts Editor and covered almost everything in his time. Had studied at U. Berkeley in California. Then went on to the Northeast and wrote many essays on Film, Dance, Music and Theatre journals before his columns appeared. A real savvy guy who knew all the arts and earned his way by building up from the ground level. Stupendous!

Artist: So do you all find your way(s) by the seat of your pants?

Theatre Critic: *(Opening the last of the envelopes)* What's this? *(He holds up a letter and then also looks at the reverse side)*

Artist: Photo of the Twin Towers going down with a mushroom cloud on the back.

FC: *(To the Artist)* Wow! Where?—when was this? What movie?

GRUEL (GREIL) MARCUS
AND ROCK CRITICISM

Influential and primary force Lester Conway Bangs was known to write his reviews of rock music on the premise of bringing the "star quotient" down to earth, and asking the most insulting of questions to begin his interviews. *The first mistake of art is to assume it's serious*, Bangs stated once in his all too short lifetime. Take here, one Greil Marcus who expounds on the serious nature of rock music and its cultural influences. Most markedly in his analysis of Bob Dylan's 1965 ground-breaking single *Like a Rolling Stone*. In fact, Marcus has written an entire book, *Like A Rolling Stone (Bob Dylan at the Crossroads)* on the history of the song. In the pantheon of rock criticism, Greil Marcus sits polar opposite to Lester Bangs.

I enter now a brief segue way into the representation of opinion in the case of **Marcus versus Bangs** (*Rock and Roll 101*).

• • •

The Signifier *(the forms a sign takes)* + **The Signified** *(the concepts that a sign represents)* **= The Sign** *(the **whole** that results from the association of the signifier with the signified).* So wrote French philosopher, linguist and semiotician Ferdinand de Saussure.

• • •

Lester Bangs once sat on stage with a New York band and wrote a review in the midst of the performance. Greil Marcus goes on the reading circuit and professes authority regarding socio-cultural *meta-isms,* mostly pertaining to the world of rock & roll and its effects. Lester Bangs was paunchy looking, and visually seemed to be on an all-nighter in any photograph taken of him. Greil Marcus has that erudite, kind of hip-scholarly look with wire-rimmed glasses and short grey hair that a lot of film critics seem to acquire. Both are Californian. Bangs from small-town Escondido, Marcus from urbane San Francisco.

Where Bangs is fairly relentless in his breaking down of the god-like status of rock stars, Marcus seems most eager to be part of the scene and presents adoring and awe-struck text. How do they both do this? The use of language. Their proximity to the subject matter. And in short, *their signage (styles).* Marcus is what you would have called a "smarty-pants" back in grade school. Bangs is the guy at the back of the classroom sleeping off a drunk or too many hamburgers and fries in his system.

Bangs impresses with his raw and instinctive wit whereas Marcus builds an argument through his exposés. Marcus is predictable, whereas Bangs is not. Bangs seems to let the music he hears approach him. Marcus, on the other hand, seems to keep it at a distance. Insisting more intelligence and intent than may actually be there in the creation of a given piece. Bangs finds

relevance. Marcus creates it. Marcus tries to find the hook of rock
& roll's relevance to society. Bangs stays clear on what the music
evokes and fails to evoke, mostly as music to a fan, not as music
meaning something other than music. Bangs seems to feel with
his thought. Marcus thinks a lot, and mostly.

Marcus is like Mick Jagger accepting knighthood from her
royal highness. Bangs is like Keith Richards saying Mick accepting
knighthood is a lot of *&%! — and not what rock & roll is about.
Marcus sounds (the sound of the name) like an emperor's first
name. Bangs sounds (the sound of the name) like he's meeting
chicks under the boardwalk somewhere in New Jersey. Perhaps de
Saussure would say one is a rock & roller. The other is a journalist
of sorts. But you know how the French are about anything
American. Especially rock & roll.

BEAUTY AT THE CAFÉ (BAD ESPRESSO 2), OR: *SEMIOTICS MY ASS!*

Speaking of signs! Five-foot-ten. Long black hair. Red lipstick, a Starbuck's latte, a dog and a yoga mat! And she sits and sits and sits and lingers totally dressed-up and looking more than her best. You have your espresso across the street. It's more organic and less pretentious there. More like a small town or European café. On your side of the street, dudes come in with half-beards and ill-fitting straw hats like Jimmy Stewart in *Mr. Hobbs Goes on Vacation.*

Is this woman waiting for bad-acting teen idol Fabian (Forte)? Is he going to sing something so oily that his teeth are gonna take on that early '60s too-hip-to-be-square radioactive gleam? Would she dig him if he went down on his eager knees and pleaded a 'Venus'-inflected croon to her goddess-ness? How many bad coffees can you have in one day waiting for this to happen? Is this a TV ad for toothpaste or shampoo? Does Dick Clark own this moment? Would Fabian dare sing *La Donna è Mobile* as an over-sound to a Mobil gasoline ad? And—who's watching who? Who's the who to watch? Is there anything left to see? What could possibly be on TV? Does DVD count as TV? Is there a way to answer that on Google? Can I text you on it? Can you get back to me? Here's the photo!

Holy cabooses! Hello Dolly! Wow, we are gonna have ourselves a big adventure. Really? Don't you have to do something more than sit at a café or Tweedledee-dee/Tweedledee-dum with your thumbs to a little black pocket machine? Don't you have to move? Isn't adventure about action versus sitting watching and talking about it? Hold it! Some guy is going over? He's not Fabian but he's got good teeth. He's carrying a Luigi Pirandello play, and resembles a European (French) professor. Looks like he's got bags of money to spend in bohemian fancy.

You're thinking you should take your organic espresso to the park. Too many dogs this time of day. Won't work. You are still sitting watching. You light a smoke. It's your last one and then you're gonna leave you tell yourself: "Yeah, just one more." Why? To see if she moves? Your semiotic curiosity is expanding and your head feels like Max Headroom's about to explode. Now there's teeth! Make the moment. It's all you got otherwise it's dogs at the park. Enter the myth.

"Hey, Mikey!" you call to a friend walking by the guy about to speak to Miss Red Lips. Everyone turns. Not because they are Mikey but because you've screamed it, but you've got her attention. She's looked up. Why? Because everybody else has. That's the key. Anonymity. There is no commitment in that for her. Wants the world's attention but careful to be viewed not giving it back. Poseur(ess)? Perhaps? But the dude looks French so they might sort it out?

Noting her zodiacal necklace he says: *Le significance de le poisson* (the significance of the fish) *c'est que le poisson est sans eau.* (is that the fish is without water). She laughs. *Kenn ah byee yeww a café?* he enquires sort of Depardieu-like, rustically. "Well, I already own one," she responds. "But yes, I would love another latte. *Sans* oh (*water*), of course." She giggles her best Alliance Française pronunciation. *Why ovv couurssse!* (who hasn't heard a Frenchman say that?). He curtseys his head, and goes in to purchase at the forever line-up/ pay first /see what you get? Starbuck's counter.

In the meantime a guy not named Mikey is sitting next to you asking for change. Taking a minute to rummage your pockets, you don't see Miss Red Lips get up and leave across the street. The French professor walks out onto the Starbucks patio. Later, at the park, you see him kicking dogs away from his well-cuffed pant-leg —a real gunslinger—two lattes in his hands with no Miss Red Lips to be seen.

THE CONSPIRACY THEORIST—
MAKE THAT "THERAPIST"

There's always a psychoanalyst ready to listen to and dissect your issues about relationships or your existential woes. Trained or not in Freudian or Jungian theory, they pride themselves on offering paradigms imported from Victorian Austria. Of course this is all grafted onto North American fear, love of family, alienation, doing better than the Jones' corporate-ism and cowboy-ism. So if you are in a session and you tell one that you dreamed of the World Trade Centre going down the night before it did, or you are old enough to say that you dreamed of John Kennedy being carried in a dark shroud—their eyes shine at the magnificent potential for really long sessions into next spring.

Soon enough, they have you thinking of your dad and ma and siblings and your rise from womb to social order. You get a feeling your chief concern shouldn't be the Towers or the health of the President but your own. Mental health that is. So you kind of agree and try not to take too many Valiums or sleeping pills to keep some sort of *homeostasis* (not Stasi) in your day and body. But you keep having these dreams of things that actually happen after you've dreamed them. You read all the qua-trained centuries of Nostradamus, and the Jungian archetypes and *Book Of Runes*.

Yet your dreams persist. It's like someone is visiting you in your sleep but you never get a chance to see who it is that's telling you all this stuff that's going to happen. But it does happen and you sit in the dark thinking there has to be some relationship between you and the world outside above the mediocre cleric job you do day to day. You know your Kafka but that doesn't help. You even bring up the great writers and philosophers to your therapist and the therapist insistent and quiet, has you cast her as part of the conspiracy to deny you sleep, and leave you in fear of losing your mind. You have determined that you are the theorist and the therapist is the therapist.

Conspiracy takes further shape. You dream that you have broken down a door and that feels good. Then you remember that the door was made of glass and you fear you might have cut someone in your rage. You didn't know it was rage before the therapist suggested it was. You got to get out of this puzzle. You never liked them as a kid. The empty spaces in the puzzle always made you feel lonely. You'd always find yourself making up images in your head to fit the puzzle but they never did. But it was certainly more fun that way. Now some of those images make up the dreams you have. The ones about the Towers and the President. They seemed to be ones you remember from childhood. You can't figure out why they recurred so close to the fact? Why you had them so early in life and then they returned? But they are the only two that ever happen. Again and again.

The therapist has heard all this from you before. Nothing she says suggests it will be any different. You don't like to think this is the way the gods cut your cards but it sure seems that way. The therapist must be in on it. It being the world of your fear. The therapist is always present. You have determined the therapist is part of the conspiracy. You wish you were on something else. You try *Moby Dick* and *Don Quixote* and your eyes grow tired of waves, harpoons and windmills.

You are hollering down at a sidewalk thirty storeys below your feet. You grab onto a flagpole. Your hands are growing blue and numb. *Jump! Jump!! Jummmp!!!* you hear the holler from the small faces below. You let go and as you bounce to rest you see that the people holding onto the fireman's safety net all have the same face. *I am home*, you say to yourself. The white frock that you see on yourself. The wheelchair. The smell of bad food. You will write a book about conspiracy theorists. You will begin after Jell-O is served. The Jell-O is lime green.

WEATHERMAN WRONG?
WEATHERMAN RIGHT?

(More Signs)

When you see the **H** on a weather map is that a symbol for a Hotel and is the **L** a symbol for fifty? *When in Rome do as the Romans do.* — which would be a lot better weather than the northern parts of the continent where this is being written from. So who was visiting Rome that gave way to that adage? Is this why Richard Nixon tried to eat with chopsticks in attempting détente with China in the 1970s? Is this what Richard Nixon, Lyndon Johnson, the Bush Clan and a whole lotta other presidents meant or mean when they decided (decide) to *circumnavigate* the globe?

The phrase actually arose when St. Augustine asked St. Ambrose, Bishop of Milan, about eating habits as the bishop was preparing for a visit to the ancient capitol in 387 **Anno Domini**.

He didn't have a weather channel. No big Hs and Ls and swirling clouds and touch-screen radar with all sorts of **allergy** medication advertisements. He might have had pigeons but what did they know? Well, the flying kind anyway? There must have been some *stoolies* nonetheless in the high (poison this guy/poison that guy) intrigue of powerful Mother church. Speaking of **immunity** ... Well, let's get to that later.

So a weatherman *(person)* can be wrong most of the time and right some of the time and working all of the time. How do you get work like that and keep it? Getting something wrong so often and still being employed? I mean, it's valiant and all to show concern for our need to know what the weather is going to be like. To be informed. Like if there's a fire in the hills and it's going to come down and burn the cornfields. Or there's a volcano erupting a few mountains over and you gotta clear the village of all goats and children.

But in the city. Do you really need to know it's raining by TV, when you can look outside or hear the clatter on your roof? What's will all the information about the kids at the park at a festival of clowns or a big barbeque reunion? Isn't it about being sold the idea that you need to know things are good? The "comfort" being sold to you by programmers? Can't we just feel the weather in the city? I mean, what did we do before all the ads and traffic reports?

Notice that whenever there is a disaster (not unlike whenever there is a political assassination) the clips are repeated *ad nauseam* to the point that we numb up and switch the channel to anything that avoids the tedium. So what is it that makes us like this kind of programming and then turn from it as if we were denying we ever engaged in watching it? I mean, a weatherperson is telling you what everybody else is telling you. Thank god they haven't decided to put a happy face on the sun icons. What would they use for thunder? The face of Zeus? Then what happens?

Should the icon be Allah or Jesus or Buddha or Jane *(who's Jane?)*? And if I'm a Jane and I'm a man, what could that be saying? Would I get a job reporting the weather because of equal opportunity? Does it matter how wrong or right I am? And what if I'm left? Like left of centre (on the map usually west)? Is west left? Is left wrong? Is left gone? And so it's Tea Party time in America. Strange with all the Starbucks and Seattle's Best that we are returning to tea. Are we talking continental Indian teas? Can we still be using the word Indian? Do they make good tea in Cleveland 'cause they got *Indians* there and they swing bats? Like Tony Soprano!

In fact, there's a new line of bats at your local sporting goods store. They have *The Canseco* (big and lies a lot all over the field), *The McGwire* (doesn't say anything), *The Barry Bond's BALCO Bat* (signed by all the lawyers it took to get him off), and *The Clemens* (with which you are guaranteed to strike out — not a great seller). So who's right and who's left? The weatherperson (man/woman) telestrates your nearest hurricane, and they swirl counter-clockwise (left to right) in the Western Hemisphere and clockwise (right to left) in the Eastern Hemisphere. Thus confusing the geo-political issue more 'cause according to the smarties at the CIA the east (right) is where all the communists are who are (left). Though a look to Central and South America coughs up a few radicals to these settings.

I mean, wouldn't it have been a treat to see Hugo Chavez give the weather report? Like a Mr. Hyde to Chauncey Gardner's Dr. Jekyll. So the vagrancy of truth continues and it looks like it's a full moon tonight. Ah oooooh! And if we close all the blinds and drapes and shut ourselves in we can avoid the simple things we already know and are available and tune in for more commercials and watch, watch, watch the experts tell us which way the wind is blowing.

MISS DOWDY VERSUS PBS

Any time I read a Dowdy commentary, I say: How did this person get the work? Doesn't matter if I don't get an answer. Then I think Camille Paglia, Anne Coulter and all the opinionated punditry and headiness of womenfolk chasing down the Gertrude Stein Prize for best hair-do. Let me say first off that my mother had hair on her legs and could lift a weight as well as any man from her southern Italian village. And you know what else? She could sing like a nightingale. And you know what else? They answered her. Now I'm not saying that's the kind of woman that impresses me. I think Stein and Sontag and Adrianne Rich and Virginia Woolf and Madame Currie, Ma Barker and Einstein's wife (what was her name?) gave it up as good as any man.

It's just the dowdiness of the present day voices passing themselves (the voices) off as expert in anything but opinion. The assumed authority of opinion by the nature of being associated to a big paper or online news site or broadcaster? Take public television. PBS in America. Why is it they present stories with an almost humble and low-key tone? Why is it they can have full-length conversations with interviewees and you actually experience insight and learning? How does a TV station do that outside of having to prod "Viewers Like You" and the donations from Bill Gates and the like? A belief perhaps? A belief that "the story" is more important than the "storyteller" (i.e.: supposed broadcast journalist)?

So Ray, Jeffrey, Judy, Jim and Gwen offer something Miss Dowdy does not. An honest face and a communication of information not intended to make them stars. You never get the feeling that's their gig. From Miss Dowdy, and others mentioned above, it's the distinct feeling you get. The star power of having a platform to mouth off from. Steroid punditry and an attempt to kick in on the fame factor associated with the camera/newspaper/radio/internet giving you a place regardless of your level of expertise.

We all have aesthetic preferences. Even for the news we watch. But why do we have such a bevy of specialty stations where years ago we accepted we only had one or two and went with it? Without the need or want to turn away from what we didn't like? $$$$ and a supposed taste for each person? The myth of individuality yet we all do the same thing. Turn the TV on, the radio on, read the papers—assume and furthermore borrow intelligence. And I have all these papers now but I don't have any walls to paint.

It's been that way for a while. People using drop-sheets or painters so good they don't use newspaper. So Miss Dowdy—sure you're there. But what do you really do? Cynical cut and paste? You can't be thinking what you offer is as important as Stein or Thomas Merton? Oh, you do. Well let's see you shave your head and sit in a monastery for sixteen or more years. Then I'll read you with faith and even charity. Just because I don't believe you intend anything but intelligence and cleverness. *Truth.* That's a whole other station. God knows there are more to come.

JUNE 31ST, THREE IN THE AFTERNOON

That was the day the moss started rolling off the rocks in Rattlesnake Park, an escarpment looking over farmland and the small towns east of the city. Year in and year out, the moss had grown there and the scent of musk and humus filled the spring air as hikers and families found their goat steps up the high incline leading to the cliffs.

The day before had been one of mourning. A kid had made plans to hike with his pal and dad and as they had taken a break they decided to stand on a ledge of rock. It gave way, taking them all to the bottom. No one survived. The mother was horrified and shocked into depression and fear. She called on her extended family and together they prayed for the loss. At church that afternoon, songs were sung and one of her nephews brought his

77

rock band as they did a punk version of *Onward, Christian Soldiers.*
There were grimaces and frowns from the older folk. The minister
hadn't been too keen on the idea but he agreed to let it go when
the mother insisted that the nephew was the dead boy's best friend.

In the front pews the closest of relatives were gathered and
Big Lloyd, the woman's younger brother, wrestled in his seat as
sweat poured down his pink-striped shirt. He had that overweight
Beach Boy look. Tanned and well fed, yet burned just a little too
much by the summer's sun. He had a welt on his right cheek. As
it was deer fly season and his new home near a creek made evenings
musty. As his kids rehearsed their Christian Punk numbers late
into the night, Lloyd found it difficult to get in a full night's sleep.
He made his money as a systems analyst for an investment firm,
his latest project being a public relations appearance by Freddy
Breecher, a financial wizard who attracted a flock through his
sermon-inflected seminars. In his mind, Calvin had it right. And
Freddy, and his followers made no mistake that Christ wanted it
Calvin's way.

Jenny, the dead boy's mom, had contemplated suicide a year
before. She had broken from her husband and dragged herself
from state to state and into Canada with her kids, her first husband
having left her for many other women (though he always said it
was one). One night, at wit's end and in the throes of a deep
depression over having caught her second (now deceased) husband
in a gay brothel, she went home and swallowed twenty pills. In the
midst of the overdose she thought to call a new man she'd met
recently. A Greek guy at an arts gathering. She always wanted to
write *the* great novel. She thought if she could just find the right
man to support her she would love him in return.

Jenny loved reading Jung. She saw archetypes in everything
and knew French half decently given the ease of travel that the
money from her first marriage allowed. The Greek guy, Johnny,

had a bipolar cousin. Only a few months back, he'd had to call the police to get his cousin Phillip taken in to protect himself and others. Johnny was recovering from his sense of betraying Phillip when he met Jenny and a night after their first meeting, Johnny had spoken about the difficulty his cousin had faced, and his own shame at having had to turn him in.

As Minister Cartwell began his sermon, Jenny sat thinking of Johnny and the poem he'd given her by Wallace Stevens titled *The Credences of Summer.* Jenny loved the airy feel of Stevens' piece. She felt it said something about her son. The blonde youth and agility and happy glow he carried. She had chosen to read a section of it for the eulogy but the pills she had to take to calm her nerves from the latest bad news left her weary and anxious.

Small towns are funny. Not in the haha sense but in the sense of gossip and everyone knowing everyone else's business. Maybe it's the open land behind the towns that makes them so gossipy as if saying everything and putting everyone in their place is a way of dealing with the forest's unknown beyond. Maybe people just get bored and turn vicious in their predicament of nothing to do but drive up to the Seven-Eleven and back again from the DVD store? One thing is certain. If you're from a small town, leave and come back, you are target number one regarding gossip. Given Jenny's history and the story of her son's death having spread, it was no surprise she felt anxious and the need to take yet another pill as Minister Cartwell started up the service. This was the day the moss started rolling off the rocks at Rattlesnake Park.

LADIES WITH DOGS / MEN WITH "FAGS"

Everyone knows that a *fag* is an old-fashioned way to say cigarette or smoke in England. All the women have dogs on my street. I have a fire-hydrant on my front lawn. I am not responsible for any of this. In fact, I woke up this morning and it was raining and I had nothing to do with that either, although I remember a few days back it was really hot and I sort of prayed for rain. Not really prayed but hoped it would. But the dogs and fags? Didn't ask for them but there they are each day on leashes and men smoking cigarettes. They all (except the fire-hydrant) meet down at the park as weekend Friday starts rolling around in spring summer and fall. They stay through the weekend, sitting and texting and barking and smoke-smoking and sometimes there are even weekend athletes playing bad tennis and "short" volleyball. By short I mean … well … by short I mean that the volleyball players seem to be from a mid-South American country. They don't really play by the rules as they palm and boot the ball over and have some thirteen players on each side of the court. I never thought volleyball was soccer with two men added, but you aren't going to get an argument from me. Not on that anyway.

What I do want to say however is that I wish people who like using parks would not let their dogs pee on the strawberry bushes. I know this is near impossible to avoid but I'd like to see it nonetheless. There are so many things to complain about and this is the one that bothers me the most. I once saw one of the volleyball players go and pee on the strawberries. I don't really have a complaint about that either. After all, a man is a man and a dog is a dog. Perhaps if the dog played volleyball I would feel different about it but the dogs always seem to want to bite the volleyball players and the ball which makes it difficult for the thin-wristed ladies who were just out preening and getting the day's air into their lungs before they have to stoop and pick up Rover's number two.

I've seen many a woman in high-heels standing tall over the volleyball men and scolding her pup while the men smudge the sweat on their stern brows. And they never say they are sorry. The dog owner ladies that is. The dogs might but they don't get a chance as they are yanked back by a dominatrix-type command to heel and walk on with their noses high in the air. Everybody seems to want the higher air. The ladies, the dogs (after pooing), the volley-ball men and even the men with the smokes. Everybody looks up sooner or later.

The most lovely thing at the park are kites. But the city fathers stopped them. Seems the wires could cut birds or strangle animals. One thing's important though. If you are looking up watch where you step.

IT'S YOU WHO LOOK DIFFERENT, NOT THE MIRROR

(Feng Shui)

Ha! You don't believe that, do you? The mirror has been a *sign* of you for as long as mirrors and you have been in existence. Water. Narcissus. Pretty hair. Male or female. Female or male. Dogs and hippopotami and alligators have a peek too though the latter don't get that good a view from under the surface. And there are days, modern days, where you can see you reflected at every turn. On a glass-building wall. In reflection off a streetcar or subway door. And the great many mirrors in underground malls that give you that roomy feeling so you don't get too claustrophobic. This is an age of mirrors. No one goes through a looking glass. There's no time for that. A reflection back at yourself takes precedence when your date is waiting or your prospective employer sits behind a desk expecting your best.

If you've ever spent time in a cabin in the woods (a la Thoreau) without many mirrors (but one to shave to), have you noticed that you don't really need a mirror as much? You are happy to look out. See the world beyond self. Listen to the rustle of wind in the trees and watch a leaf course its way to autumn ground. What do you look like at these moments? What do you look like not seeing your reflection back to you in reverse? It is in reverse, you know. Everything in a mirror is. Perhaps that's why we feel twinned to something in this universe? It starts with you.

Put then a TV monitor in front of yourself. A glass one. Don't turn the TV on. Look into it. There is nothing but a kind of out-of-focus, vague you. The minute you turn the monitor on you disappear. You do not enter the monitor as many advertisers would like you to. Having you feel you are now surfing or eating lobster in Cancun like everyone else seems to be. Ah, that lobster and the skinny-dipping. Where is the beer bottle invented that has a mirror on it? But this is not a time for sales and marketing. I'm certain someone will come up with that in time. Mirrors give you pain.

Mirrors give you pleasure. They give you laughs and tears and good and bad teeth. They give you naked. They give you winter clothes. They give you company yet in a strange way if you are actually standing there alone—you don't feel quite as alone unless you are holding in your hand a book by Nietzsche or Kant. And even more so if you hold the book up over your head or in front of your face and the writing is backwards. So much for *Überman*. Superman comics don't look good in mirrors. Somehow Batman comics do. And The Flash. He moves at the speed of light and can go right through a brick wall or a mirror. What to do with all that speed? *Help me Albert!* (Einstein!)

There are concave mirrors pulling your image in. There are convex ones pushing your image out. There are magnified mirrors in case you want even more of yourself. Or if you don't the dentist does. A good smile can make a mirror worthwhile. There are mirrors smashed and mirrors put back together. Though your image may come back a little shardy, it is still you, perhaps matching how you feel inside. And for further company, there is the triptych mirror. A bit of right, a bit of left and then you square (or oval) right in the centre. If we removed every mirror, would we be forced to run to the nearest lake for a sight of ourselves? Could we trust it when someone says we're looking good or feel disheartened if someone said we were not looking so hot? How would we prove either?

The mirror is a sign of you. Alligators and deep water dwellers aside, there's a howling in the woods. But that's another story. The image that a sound creates. But for now, just look at you, you, you!

NEIL

(The Name is the Same)

Neil One

"*Hot August night . . .*" goes the tune and the deer flies are buzzing to this American song about a revival tent in the Southeast. You feel like you are at the beginning of something. It's the geography in this Neil Diamond tune from the late '60s. He does his 'Hallelujahs' and conjures up the crowd arriving at a gospel evening. What you are not sure of is whether the folks gathering —and for that matter—the character's voice ND has created is African-American or Caucasian.

We are taken with experience. Sometimes our own. Sometimes those of others that we merely witness and are moved by. In the world of political correctness there are tricky fault lines our attraction to "other" has to navigate. Paul Simon takes heat though includes musicians from South Africa on his landmark mid-80s album *Graceland*. The music press hounds him and the African-American community feels he has not the authority to go so deeply into a kind of sacred material. Not that there was a revolt by boxers when his '60s hit *The Boxer* came over the airwaves. We did not know whether the boxer in the story was African-American, Latino or Asian-American. We could assume that boxers in general were unlikely to use phrases like *"squandered my resistance for a pocketful of mumbles, such are promises."*

Still we did gather insight into the experience of being a down-trodden, loser-type boxer looking back on his failed career. How did Simon declare for himself the right to speak/sing on this issue? One will argue that "race" is a different matter. But to tell you the truth I never heard much from the African-American music community (from Motown to Neverland) about Ladysmith Black Mambazo or Hugh Masekela (the latter did have an instrumental hit somewhere along the '60s) before Simon's work.

Was it an issue of jealousy? That someone in the African-American community didn't think of it first. Especially on the heels of Mandela being released from prison? Did Simon (an old hand at the music hits game) take advantage of black South Africans and their music? Prior to this we had Dylan Zimmerman singing the story of Joey Gallo, with many a supposed quote from Joey and others. I do not recall any great hoopla from the Italian-American community that a Jewish-American singer was infringing on their experience, rights or "zone." If anything it felt glory that one of their own was mythologized. So why was Paul Simon demonized? And why weren't Dylan Bob and Neil Diamond? Envy? Their exploitative versus creative natures? Did Italian-Americans and Asian-Americans jump happily in their seats at Spike Lee's interpretation of Italian and Asian-Americans in his *Do The Right Thing* from the same period?

I remember buying that Neil Diamond album back when the Beatles had just broken up. That wasn't the reason I bought it. I liked his voice. Was curious about his sound. Though I knew I was listening to a pop-song, not reading Thomas Wolfe or Jack Kerouac. There was appeal enough to try the album out. And that song, *Brother Love's Traveling Salvation Show,* opened the window on joy, belief and enthusiasm for experience, firstly not my own, and secondly, for its ability to "geographize" somewhere I hadn't been. In short, I became interested in gospel music through the son of a cantor.

• • •

Neil Two

Neil, as in Young, was coming out with Crosby, Stills and Nash close to the same period. Now here was a Neil who sang off key and looked wired to his head zone with a lament and lilt of a man looking at the world from his basement apartment window. Not quite a poet (in the Dylan Bob) sense — (who was?) but a peculiar intensity nonetheless and a *one-of-the stoners* style and sound. His *weirdness* as opposed to Neil Diamond's slickness was distinct. But he never hit me the way Steve Stills (his counterpart) in CSN&Y did. A truly gifted songwriter and vocalist/blues player, Stills wrote the most enervating of the collective's songs.

Neil's essence was his subtlety. Another singer in the background who balanced the pulse and push of Stills' work. The interior voice to Stills' expansive and extroverted long-song forms. As Young continues with his sorties with later generation bands such as Pearl Jam and writes a protest CD, there's more of a country gentleman Spanish-hat feel to him than a relevant creative force. He is not Dylan Bob. Nor John Mellencamp for that matter. No matter how much grunge he conduces from his electric as an overgrown hobbit.

• • •

Neil Three

Of the two, Neil Diamond and Neil Young, I wonder which Neil Neil Armstrong would have played on that flag-waving moon half a century ago? My bets are on Diamond. Star-spangled with *Sweet Caroline* blasting across space and into our TV monitors. Songs that play between goals and touchdowns matter in America and on the moon.

CRITICS WHO KNOW JACK

(Some Words on Rock & Roll Poetry)

I think it was 1969 or so. I came across a fantastic little book entitled *The Poetry of Rock* edited by Richard Goldstein, one of those New York *Village Voice* types who seemed to be in the vanguard of the discussion about the poetic value of the rock song lyric of the day.

It didn't hurt his case any, given that you had a decade of Dylan and Beatles albums that took their reference points and image foundations from everything from the stylizations of French symbolist and surrealist traditions and American Beat poetry to suggestions of Edward Lear, the metaphysical poet Thomas Dekker (as in "Sleep Little Wanton—don't you cry.") and a slew of other writers that predated the grand and vibrant cultural explosion of the decade.

There were many other books that came about. Wonderful ones that weighed more heavily on the *content of the rock artists' works rather than on the aspect of their celebrity.* Young men and women who were studying journalism or in some cases graduate journalism courses or journalism dropouts. Writing criticism on the tunes of the day and their cultural effect. Yet these young critics had no gain in mind except the sharing of insight and realization that the songs of the period were pulling on cultural manifestations that existed long before the Les Paul, Stratocaster, Rickenbacker, Martin, Gibson and Guild fell into the hands of Eric Clapton, Dave Davies, Roger McGuinn, Jimi Hendrix and Frank Zappa.

These young critics actually understood that when Ray Davies led The Kinks with his song *Dedicated Follower of Fashion*, with the words: *They seek him here. They seek him there...*, he was pulling a reference out from *The Scarlet Pimpernel* published in 1905, written by transplanted Hungarian Baroness Emma Orczy, about a dandy highwaymanish English fop who masked himself in dual identity. They knew there was a lineage being formed from Emerson and Whitman to Kerouac and Ginsberg and The Beats to Robert Bobby Zimmerman Dylan.

They knew Syd Barrett and the rest of Pink Floyd had a raw yet keen sense of art and architecture and applied it to soundscaping some of their finer albums.

They knew Zappa pulled his satirical constructs into full bloom by listening to the modernist Edgard Varèse and guessed that Procol Harum's lyricist Keith Reid probably dropped acid reading Chaucer's *Tales* before sitting down and hitting the track *Whiter Shade of Pale.*

But for a handful of self-important types such as Greil Marcus and Robert Christgau at *The Voice*, the love of the "newness in word to song" and its relationship to the past in literature, music and art in general, created a groundwork for the fusion of what we call today, *the marriage of high art to popular culture.*

So why did this marriage occur? Art school pimple-headed teenagers tired of 'O' levels and toothy teen idols? Somewhat, yet how did the *writers of the songs shift* the music industry paradigm from propping up made-up pre-karaoke-doll boy or girl singers to actually writing, composing, producing, recording and performing "their own work"?

Well, one could say literature and the arts lay sleeping in academe and the music of the '50s was "lying" about the real spirit of *expression*. With the early sixties, the line shifted to the writers of songs expressing their own work as opposed to interpretation of their work by others. A big shift in originality of song to the voice of its creator(s).

The Stephen Foster mould formed in the 19th century where the *first real American songwriter* with a sustained body of work, having his material sold to minstrel show producers for measly sums and over-produced gloss distortions of his beautiful Schubertian and post-colonial melodies with words of celebration and tragedy, *was finally broken.*

One point rarely discussed in the wonder of the time in which The Beatles, Bob Z Dylan, The Rolling Stones and others created their work was the issue of *creative* power. And given the political intensity of the time, power became central to most of these artists as they moved along into the teeth of the music industry. What gave them a 'core' power as a result of performing their own work was recognition and the growing degree of $$$ that royalties spawned.

Because the royalties and performing rights increased (though there were vultures at every turn) the *power of identity* could not be denied. The power of *"who* it was that was saying *what."* The power of this self-expression on such a mass and media-propulsed scale inspired the world on a grand and accessible level. *Being an artist with **something to say** meant something out there.*

And so even to a greater degree, today the artist has become relatively independent from the control mechanisms challenging his or her creative power. Still, the question of standards remains. The open market of independency in all the arts brings back to focus the *value of expertise* regarding editing and other aspects of broker-ship in the arts across the board. But the impulse for artists to develop and perform original work is greater, not only in numbers but in part as a result of the "artistic and cultural" creators going to deeper aesthetic ground. Though some of its members have gone to the lightness of corporate mega-musicals and New Age simpledom.

And there are many examples where artists, once at the forefront, have made of themselves corporate entities. Point to one Paul McCartney who in the 1990s released a book of poetry *Blackbird Singing*. With the British Poet Laureate Andrew Motion writing the preface, the Liverpool Knight fundamentally "bought" his way to aesthetic high ground. It seems that in McCartney's case the richness of his song lyric was either under the influence of John Lennon or an innovation in songwriting that *was of a time* and that even if T.S. Eliot and e.e. cummings were to come back from the dead and write accolades about his attempt to write serious verse, even they, with their poetic range and acumen, would never find in McCartney's *serious poetry* attempt, the rich originality and aesthetic intrigue than they would in the highly crafted work of this once Beatle's song lyric.

Fastforward >> So Eminem. Letters backwards. Feel like I want to listen to what he says. Rap. Secret societies. Codes of language. Good luck breaking them and admire, admire, admire. The old aesthetic versus meaning argument. But he's talking lots. Lyric driven! Words make Music!!!!

Rock & roll has done one thing for certain. It has made kings of clowns. The courts are upside down and have been for some time. Witness Bono and his sitting with Heads of State and to us the clown is the Head of State, not the clown. And good luck getting in. It's a dirty old Nick Caraway world where you see the thing bought and bought and bought. But maybe a clown? Maybe a Bono? Maybe a Springsteen? An Eminem with the e backwards *is the result of the lyric.* The *integrity of the lyric. The composition of word as much as music?* And that turns the political cranks of the mega music giants and the *wanters of association* to the freedom the lyric expresses.

Yes there has always been a place for poets but one must remember Bob Robert Zimmerman's offering that *"poets drown in lakes."*

Or Bob! THEY PUT A GUN TO THEIR HEADS. — COBAIN.

Expression through words and music is some powerful stuff! It might just show you what you didn't want to know more than showing anything to anyone on the outside listening. Then you throw it back to Chuck Berry and Little Richard. It's always good to be a pioneer. Seems you have an in-built sense of struggle and take the road as it comes without the self-destruct. MAKE THE ROAD and sing happy and pretty into kingdom come!

TATTOOS

*B*ut that which was most remarkable in the appearance of this splendid islander was the elaborate tattooing displayed on every noble limb. So Herman Melville writes as Ishmael narrates his introduction to the character Queequeg in *Moby Dick*'s opening chapters. Tattoos have long served humans. From fashionable henna to drunken ruddy sailors, back to fashion again, there are few symbols or *signs* that are permanent and open to interpretation, no matter how clear the wearer was when he or she had the work done.

Is it a peculiar thing to mark one's skin? Is there a sense of Eros in the titillating needle buzz that is almost a sort of *injection rub*? A high and an escape from the skin you are born with? Or a deep externalization of your *within* becoming *without* (in the Hindi sense)?

My father had a tattoo. Actually had two but the one that you couldn't miss was the one you would see at family picnics. The lady on his chest. She must have been put on before he met my mother who I'm certain would have stopped him from doing it. The lady looked like a bad version of a One-Eyed-Jack, head sideways and even more one-dimensional. Little expression on her face and pretty tough-looking. She was not a pin-up by any means. Perhaps the submarine tattoo artist was drunk and he had another *guy* pose for the work? That said and guessed at, my dad had her all his life. Jiggling when he took a shower or swam and getting partly tanned in summer when he wore a low V-neck T-shirt.

The more interesting tattoo was the one on his right hand. Three dots. I always thought it might have been a *die* face as my dad did like to gamble. What I liked about it is that I had no idea (but guessing) at what it really symbolized. They were not three in a row on a diagonal like it would be on a die. They were more triangular. Maybe the three corners of the Sicilian island close to his hometown in southern Italy? Maybe they were practice dots that the artist put there to see if my dad liked his work before he inked the big girl on his chest? Could it be a secret membership? Was it he and his two brothers? What were these marking on his right hand between the forefinger and thumb?

I think of those dots when I walk along the streets of my neighbourhood and see the florid and grotesque markings a younger generation has chosen. I also think of Bruce Dern's madness in the film *Tattoo* where he drugs Maude Adams after kidnapping her and tattoos her as she sleeps. Needless to say, she is a touch horrified in the morning when she awakens to hear him speak of the brilliance of his art. The perfection of his art on her smooth white body. Then there are the tattoos from the Nazi concentration camps. Markings of a paranoid yet deliberate madness. A branding that has left its mark on human nature for time immemorial.

Dad's now passed away. I regret never taking a photograph of "his lady." Ones of him with my mother must suffice.

MARGINALIA

Sounds like a type of bug disease? Look at your daily papers and then your internet adverts and see how much is not the main news of the day? Even if the Middle East is burning and the Arabic world is lighting up with revolt, the almost dominant feature in most papers either via net or print is the cacophony of ads ads ads that fill in the sides and bottoms and tops and windows inside windows of pages selling and alerting you of the nothings that want your every attention.

Is it so desperate a situation that we need to be bombarded and then set up fire-walls and spam filters to get away from the dredge and glut? Why such an un-holistic environment through which to experience word and image and the pleasure of knowledge and opinion? Ads sell newspapers and online services. And you pay for the distraction? And then you choose the route of selectivity yet by the time you have done this, it may be true you have filtered much out but your fatigue from the effort leaves you little juice to enjoy what you thought you were pursuing. Intelligent, un-gossipy story lines and information about the world around you.

Remember *Mad Magazine* and cartoonist Sergio Aragones' little off-beat drawings in the margins? How you read the main satirical take on the latest movie and then your eyes wandered to the margins and saw little men falling off ladders into vats of sharks with American flags (a satire on Iwo Jima)?

This is not to argue that *The New York Times* or other dailies of that substantial ilk carry only dregs. This is to argue that what is valid and intriguing in reportage is watered-down to a fashion and "fatted-cow-ness" culture that tries to evoke in you domestic needs beyond your *needs* and even more succinctly, means. Try something to get this point across. Take the Bible, any version. Set the stories of the Old and then New Testaments on pages with enough room for the selling of jewellery and vacuum cleaners and TVs and the like in the margins. Let all the stories of joy and horror sit along the trivial mechanisms of the sales machinery. Try staying focused, as in Revelations the Horsemen of the Apocalypse come down in a rain of fire, and not see the sparkling diamond on a well-toned ankle leading to a fascinating knee and high skirt-line in the margins. Do you at this point think of Sodom and Gomorrah or can you read on about what each of the Four Horsemen actually do? Would there be greater clarity (less distraction) in a Catholic catechism, though generalist, still morally more "pure" and honest?

Some would argue we are already in Sodom and Gomorrah and waiting for the salt and crash of our great capitalist edifices. The Moloch of ancient Sanskrit literature (the god that devoured the young) as referenced in Allen Ginsberg's *Howl*.

Recently I had the joy of meeting up with an old ball-hockey pal. He has always been sporty and a great hockey goalie though his dreams of the professional life of an athlete did not come to fruition. Instead he became a tool-dyer's assistant, never really learning the trade but choosing instead to live a small town life and rediscover the words of the Bible which he was introduced to at a young age. He now believes we are in the "end times" and disses the days he listened with intrigue to Pink Floyd and Led Zeppelin.

That is all now "devil stuff" and he watches videos of modern day pseudo-prophets telling of the evils all around us. He believes *Stairway to Heaven* to be hedonistic and born of the influence of Satan. His anti-capitalist stance is interesting. However, for him it requires narrowing down his fields of education and exploration of the differences within most people. He now has set his target and belief that all energy must be directed to God, yet when I saw him last he wore a Bob Marley T-shirt. I dared not ask him about his understanding or knowledge of Rastafarian culture and religion. I dared not ask because I feared the total loss of one of our true connections — the joy of rock & roll music. I found though that he was willing to talk of Bob Marley and the lyrics in his songs. He didn't offer that Marley's religious beliefs were a distraction and a movement away from God.

Sometimes you sense when not to go into certain subject matter. Open though the person you might have contention with might seem, you may be better off talking hockey scores. The changes in people you love can be devastating. By the end of our day together, he insisted that his mind was now clear and that each man, woman or child is "free" to choose their belief systems but that the God *he believed in* was the *only* right path. That we were born with free will but in no way was that will ever right in believing in a greater spirit unless it was the Christian God of the Bible. The Christ. The Nazarene. The Jewish prophet who confronted his own people, because as my pal said: *Christ's people (the Jews) were wrong.*

I don't know why my hockey pal loads his life up with long odds, but loyalty is one of his greatest character traits. Right or wrong—he will always believe in what he chooses to. The lack of challenge and critical thought he has towards his own beliefs, however, is an issue of concern. Fading are his love of hockey statistics and card collecting. He wishes one day to go to Jerusalem. Because Christ worked his missions there. Not because it is the foundational geographic local of Islam, Christianity and Judaism. The religions outside of his interpretation of Christianity have been relegated to the margins. Would I had Aragones' last instalment in *Mad*. In fact, if I can leave this for a moment, I think I will go to the newsstand and see what I can find.

LYRIC INTERPRETATION

(With No Help from My Friends)

Songs mean something sometimes. And sometimes they don't. Sometimes the writer intends them to mean something. And often, even if he or she meant something, they don't feel they should explain the song as much as they might speak of the experience of writing songs *per se*. This "keeping your cards close to your chest" has caused many a complication in lyric interpretation. It is also often interpreted as obfuscation, which in the end seems pretty harsh judgment by listeners who cannot break the hermetic seal of many a complexly written song.

I consider as I write this that the least difficult songs to interpret are the campfire songs taught to children (i.e.: *One, two three O'Leary ...*), and songs of protest (towards something external, that is). Ones like *The boss don't pay no money* . . . type protest songs. Come to think of it. Who was *O'Leary*? (But I'll get to that later.)

One striking example of song interpretation came a few years back at a Festival of World Music. A performer from Latin America was singing a song about burning down a rich man's house but only Spanish speaking listeners in the audience knew what he was saying. I asked the promoter if he found it strange that people who didn't understand the song's intent and meaning were dancing no less than they would to a Beach Boy song (for the fun of the music)? Whether the detachment from the song meaning (both in music and in lyric) made him feel awkward? I suggested he at least have lyrics available as handouts or put a translation on a screen that people could read—almost like a subtitle—to allow for deeper appreciation and understanding of the work.

He thought it was a good idea yet said there were no more funds for putting a screen up and hiring a translator. Thus what you had in the audience were listeners *vacationing* to foreign sounds without buying a ticket and getting on a plane. This I always find akin to being in Havana and hearing folks from middle-America enthuse at the five hundredth strain of *Guantanamera*, the poem by José Martí transposed into an unofficial national anthem. "Oh, listen, they are playing "Cuantammerah," the lady sipping her mojito insists. "It's not Cuant-am-mah-er-ah, Mom," her purple-haired sons corrects. "You don't even know how to say it!" "Well, you're the one who dropped out of Spanish class!" she shoots back. "There's no point in talking to you!" he says, and walks off to the beach in a huff.

Meanwhile, the mother turns back to a singing quartet and smiles, nodding her head and jostles her shoulders in approval. As she sits there, a white-shirted city local with a moustache and slicked-back hair moves in and says: *Dju laike da song—Miss?* She hasn't been called Miss for twenty-five years. And hasn't been talked to in a charming manner for almost as many. It turns out he's from Serbia and only a local because he has fled his homeland and is trying to make ends meet by working the streets. He is the Eastern European taken as a Mexican who is really only a Spanish actor like Javier Bardem in the Coen brothers' *No Country for Old Men*, but he doesn't know it. There is more music and, as the two swoon over what they don't know about each other, the boy comes back and yells at his mother: "You're such a nerd and goof! I'm leaving!" And he does.

Back to the festival promoter. — "We'll see if we might get some extra budget funds for the word screen next year. I think they use one in opera, right?" "Yes, they do. Playwright Bertolt Brecht used one for his theatrical presentations but that's another story. He used it for alienation. To break the proscenium arc of traditional theatre." "Wow, how do you know that?" "Well, I wasn't there but there are books and performances of his work ..." "Yeah, what's his name again?" "Brecht, B R E C H T — a German Marxist playwright." "Neat, I'll look him up," he responds eagerly, as the Latin American folk-singer yelps another line about taking torches to the dictator's palace.

Songs mean something sometimes. And sometimes they don't. Sometimes people just want to dance and sometimes people want to burn down palaces. All signs of a "normal" world. Or, better put, the world we have. And yes, before I segue out — *One, two, three, O'Leary...* — Who was O'Leary? I don't know? Maybe an IRA captain? I'm gathering O'Leary was Green. Doesn't sound Orange to my ear.

THE IMAGE THAT A SOUND CREATES

Screen projectors used to rattle, and before you even saw an image related to the sound of the moving picture, that hum and rattle created a sense of "what was coming"—an exuberance of sorts—an expectation! In those moments sound created images of imagination.

An airplane cracks Mach One as you are walking home from work and you can't see the plane. You think of the last vacation you took to Florida or Europe and the faces of the passengers and the manner in which you rushed to make sure you had packed everything you needed. You still can't see the plane, but the sound has created a bevy of images. An aural signifier.

In reverse. You take an early morning walk and the full moon is hanging over the houses and trees. The moon (as far as you know) makes no sound. But you recall the whispers of your loved one from a previous encounter. At that time the moon seemed to *hum* in its waxing, and *mute* itself as it waned. But the moon neither hums nor mutes.

You sit in front of your television set and begin the sorting of channel by channel to avoid the onslaught of images and sound that distract you from engaging in the narratives of certain TV programs or newscasts. You are arduous in your intent to find something interesting to watch but you become aware of your fingers and the illusion of power that you can control your viewing. You look further at your fingers and ask yourself if you haven't something better to do? Question? For all its commercial enthusiasm can TV programming create tedium and boredom? Can it offer comfort? Is it a contemporary hearth, easing you into the late evening and preparing you for your dreams and rapid eye movement?

Think of fire. Think of fire's aroma. Now you have an olfactory experience that enthuses your senses in the moment and for the most part allows a recall of the last time 'round this pleasantry. Now you realize you can have both — the power of your fingers (or the illusion of power to control your viewing) and — the pleasure of a fire in the fireplace. So with the wood crackling and wood smoke rising, the plane flying overhead (unseen), the moon hanging over the eaves, your senses are filling though you feel sleep just around the corner. Then — a car scoots down your street and the big box sound of heavy rap throws your heart up to your throat. All peace gone as you wait for the car to get to the end of the street and fade into the neighbourhoods beyond. You imagine some idiot kids making noise for fun.

The truth is, a young woman's driving home from a party but you only find this out in the morning news as you read of a car smashing into a traffic post. In your head, you hear the sound of her smash-up. You are not surprised as the sound of the music the night before seemed ready to "explode" somewhere, somehow. Sound and image. Image and sound. But *you did not expect* it to be the woman who worked at the coffee shop and smiled each morning with a happiness and flair for easy conversation.

WHERE POETS FIGHT

(Whitman, McCrae, Rimbaud)

There are numerous schools in the American system of education named after the Civil War poet, Walt Whitman. As a poet of the transcendentalist movement, Whitman with Ralph Waldo Emerson and Henry David Thoreau opened the spiritual heart of the United States and explored alternatives to denominational belief systems — i.e.: Puritanism, Protestantism arenas — and challenged belief in God for material gain.

Whitman's well-known *Leaves of Grass* with "Song to Myself" may have, or may appear, a fundamentally vain title. That is if you withdraw the meta-language. The metaphor. The working of Whitman from man to myth and the intoxication of the landscape in his pantheist nature. Like Emerson and Thoreau, finding himself alone in the vastness of the American soul made the difference between unique insight into spiritual/visceral experience and experience dictated by forces above (God). There is prayer in Whitman but not in the traditional sense. Prayer for him is honouring the wonder of the land and the people who inhabit it.

The breadth of the landscape and the movement of souls within it, be it war and industry or love, became the vital centre of Whitman's Bohemia. Weary, fatigued and almost beatified by his own intuition, Whitman was the precursor to the American Beats of the late 1950s and early '60s. To be down-trodden and in doubt. To be hurt and full of both psychological and physical pain was human. And perhaps the landscape and sense of wonder and intrigue could help heal the guns of brotherly war. Whitman, by all accounts, worked as a field nurse during the war. He did not take up arms but tended to those injured in battle. His recordings (his poems) of the atrocities of war sit alongside his celebration of "self"—America which is hard to believe is the same country.

There is little of the Republican in Walt Whitman. And as an artist of his time, perhaps more left than the Jeffersonian Democrats before and after him. His "fight" was for freedom of the spirit. He was Woody Guthrie before the 1930s dustbowl. And he was not as contained as Thoreau and Emerson. They were more the philosophers of transcendentalism. He as a poet, the spirit and the soul of it. His popularity vast as compared to the two. A combination of populism and soul of substance.

• • •

John McCrae, the Scots-Canadian best known for "In Flanders Fields," was a traditionalist poet. His sentiment, though unique to the moment, is full of platitude, does little to inject the reader with a sense of catastrophe of war. He is the West Point bugle rooting out *Taps* for the umpteenth time. Though this time in Belgium and the loss of Allied sons, he is still asking us for vengeance and to "take up the torch." For him, we must remember war and why we fought it and honour the men who gave their lives. The polar opposite to Whitman looking for a healing spirit and a desire to render war unnecessary and celebrate the higher aspects of the American conscience. To acknowledge the hurting of a country by its own violence within.

In McCrae, we have a poem akin to high school reverence with not even a hint that war just might not be a good idea. "In Flanders Fields" is a justification. It, in fact, always wants and needs the dead to exist as a cultural expression. Whitman, on the other hand, tries to find the sleeve between the damage and the progression out of it by transcendence. Making in his paradigm an argument against the nature of human violence.

• • •

French symbolist poet Jean Arthur Rimbaud wrote close to the same period America was in its Civil War. A child of a small French village, his poetry garnered attention for its vivid articulation of the disorientation of the senses. A cultural aesthetic—synesthesia—where revelation into experience and imagination came through perspectives that did not rest any laurels or depended on the laying of wreaths. No one had to die for Rimbaud's poetry to achieve its stature. Breaking away from the traditional French Academy, Rimbaud "sensed" his way into psychological terrain very few poets ever have. How could a child of sixteen, and a young man in turn, turn the mind into a cacophony of dissonance and dissension?

The excitation in Rimbaud's work stems from a non-acceptance of the norms of traditional verse and aesthetic impulse. When one reads Rimbaud, it is confrontation through which he seems to gain his trajectory. From early more conventional poems through to "A

Heart Under a Cassock" on towards the "Illuminations," he strips away at his denominational small town French Catholicism and by the time of "The Drunken Boat" has journeyed great distance from the horror of colonial France.

In contrast to Whitman, Rimbaud is not a man of inner peace. There is no wholesome intent. There is no "greater" America to be discovered and experienced as in *Leaves Of Grass*. In Rimbaud there is spite and revulsion at small-minded, small-townish-ness and its repressive nature. In short, Arthur Rimbaud sets out to un-cloister himself and his mind and pursue an unarticulated paganism. But his true release is to wander and experience even at the cost of madness. Here though, there is such a structural technique that precedes his "madness" that his target of doing away with traditional concepts of forms of thinking and imagining comes to clarity. Anything that constrains the mind and its ability to feel is the enemy.

Unlike Whitman, Rimbaud has no mythology to enter. Nor one he wishes to embrace. His "fight" is for survival. And, as I write this, I highly doubt that many schools in the French education system are named for him. His fight was to fly the coop of the Academy and produce a poetry with no aesthetic precedent. Though there are aspects of Rimbaud's challenge to the Academy in the works of his contemporary Baudelaire, and later Antonin Artaud, he was a much younger man than they when his most vibrant verse was created.

In his later years Rimbaud took on the vocation of gun-runner to Algeria and North Africa. There was little doubt that this choice of "occupation" had much to do with not giving *la merde* for his native France. So as we have an optimism with Whitman and over-dedication with McCrae, Rimbaud is a poet of abandon and contempt. All fighters—all against a different foe. Poets who fight do not rest with war. Nor with peace.

AN INTERVIEW WITH ROCK STAR ROBERT ALLYN

Q: Welcome. Your conversion to Christianity? How did it come about?

A: Conversion?

Q: Yeah, your conversion from . . .?

A: Well, we don't wanna talk about that, do we? I know it's your interview and magazine. You tell me. What's it like to have had a magazine for this many years?

Q: Robert? Can I call you Robby? Robert, what was it that gave you a sense that things had to change with your music?

A: Things change. But they don't really change, you know? They don't change like the seasons. Not unless you're an Eskimo.

Q: So it feels like you just built on where you were coming from?

A: You build but you don't really build, you know? Unless you're a bricklayer. You don't really build, you know.

Q: In your song, you sing: *You may be a bricklayer working on a home* *... You* seem to be calling to a higher place. A place where all is answered by servitude. Is that a biblical draw?

A: Cain and Abel weren't really brothers, you know. At least I heard that they weren't.

Q: And in your new recording, you touch on that. Is there something you want us to understand about the biblical stories and the present day state of our culture?

A: Well, I don't wanna say I was the first one ... couldn't be. There musta been someone, somewhere who said them stories. They need to be got down and said. You can't pretend, you know?

Q: But when you say: *Nobody's gotta fight the rain. The rain it knows your name...,* do you mean you can't twist the truth. It's inevitable?

A: Yeah, who said that? *My eyes can't twist the truth. They need no legislation...*

Q: Barry McGuire. In "Eve of Destruction."

A: Barry who? He stole my song. What a great line!

Q: Did you sue?

A: I guess. You know, there's something greater available.

Q: Are you saying: *Beware. There will be judgment!*

A: Yeah, I mean you just can't go on. Look at Lennon. He tried and what did it get him. You gotta serve.

Q: Do you think you'll ever write an opera?

A: I could, you know. I mean I could if ... well. I could if you wanted one. If you wanted but if I can't I'd find someone to write one for you, you know.

Q: Will you still be writing, say five years from now?

A: Someone's got to. Yeah, maybe it will be me. Hard to say. I mean I don't wanna say.

Q: Is there anything you'd like to tell your fans? Any advice?

A: Good luck. You know. No envy. No time to lose. Good luck. Ha!

DOES THE SNAKE WILL THE SHEDDING OF ITS SKIN?

T his wonder of ophiology. This slider and creeper and giver of apples. This 'anacondic' choker and all 'round rattler is known to shed its skin and once in a while make a good light jacket or belt or boots. When does the snake decide to let its skin go and help the accessories and fashion market kick in its new season?

Eve? Such a lovely in the catechism yet so weak and complying in her nature. A wicked vamp that changes the direction of man's fate from his ease, appointed by Heaven to thrive in glory and eternal bliss. Why this Eve? Because of a snake? A serpent? An air-licker? A bringer-down of empires? Let me loosen my belt ... If she crossed the line — really sinned — what does that say about her? And more so, about the snake? Is it possible the snake was merely sliding towards the apple and Eve saw the slide. Took it as a sign? Had she never seen an apple before that moment in the Garden? Was there absolutely nothing metaphysical going on? Was the snake maybe more interested in a worm in the apple? Was it skin-shedding time and he was rolling tree to tree to find the best place to slip into new spring wardrobe?

I can only answer that questions linger. And they linger whether I want them to or not. One small fault in a will-less woman seems to have comforted many a man and woman over the centuries. For that matter was she without will? And was the snake, and its Maker? If the Maker had a will, why do we assume the snake did not? I almost wish that in my agnostic self these questions had no place. I have no reason to doubt the existence of a Maker. However, I have no need to believe a snake has will and a woman and a man in a garden either. It all counts, I say. I accept the will to good and I accept the will to evil. That someone oversees all this is compelling. And I have no interest in loitering in a purgatorial dilemma. But did the snake shed its skin by its own design? And, were snakes on the Ark when Noah set out? Two of everything, right? Sounds like Charles Darwin to me coming back from some far-off island. Was Darwin just Noah shedding his skin?

• • •

The guy at the corner of my street is yelling: *God is all! Avoid temptation! The day is coming! Repent! It's not too late brothers and sisters!* I wince. Is it the volume of his voice? The aggression of his warnings? Or is it the great odds he faces as the restaurants and bars prepare for the evening's Babylon that cause this wince?

The hawk flies at noon, I think to myself as I recall my last visit to a cabin in the woods. It waits for the highest of suns before it glides and gyrates upwards for its call. I have never seen a hawk's egg. I have listened to its "Creep! Creep!" call and turned my eyes down to the autumn leaves that hold back no song. From whispering leaves, twirling to their rest, to owls and wolves securing the night, no sound comes close to this on the corner, rendering the pavement with fear and loathing. There is never a laugh from this man. A smile once in a breath to relieve his ingestion and exhalations.

He is as much tortured as he is in the state of revelation and epiphany. Given the time of year, he has a bushel of apples and is offering them as a representation and reminder of sin. The food bank is down the road and is waiting for him to leave his post. He usually leaves the apples behind as he has many books and paraphernalia to carry home. His relentless belief to instil horror makes the honking of horns blasting from passing cars, a balm. He knows no season but the one of hell, of salvation. One and the same. Un-separated by turn of weather. And he seems to have no one he returns home to which hastens his step in an odd way. His life is a sacrifice to belief. Whether distortion or truth, his life is being given to something "outside his own skin."

Shortly it will be evening. His interest in you will return after a rest on a rotting cot and a piece of cheese to eat. He will be given bread by the Korean Christian at the convenience store who recites a line of bible verse in a nearly sing-song rhythm with glee. Nothing stipulates that the pain of Christ not be saluted with joy. Yet whether he (the Christ) was to return or not, our boisterous friend would. This is guaranteed. In the hour he has taken to have that piece of cheese and rest, a small dog is circling in the space the man calls his corner. The dog sniffs. He squats on his hind legs. He is about to do number two when at the last second a high-heeled woman in lingerie yells: "Christ! Not on the street Mickey!" — and heads for the close-by park.

An hour or so later our Christ-talker seems to have come pre-pared. He throws some powered soap detergent onto his space and

with a scrub brush, goes to his knees and cleanses the spot where
Mickey stood. Mickey returns there with his owner every day at
the same time. His owner says the same thing every time. The day
that Mickey's owner and the Christ-talker were married, Mickey
peed on the church steps as he waited for the service to end.
Mickey has a limp from his right front paw. He usually barks at
strangers but, when he crosses the corner where street salvation is
offered every day, he stops and hisses first then moves in for his
dog-ly matters. In this, the woman is never blamed. Instead, police-
men offer rides and whistle. Young and old men alike gawk. And
pigeons flutter without the voice of doves.

HELIUM WORLD— "HOLY CRACKERS!"

(The Bee Gees, Robert Plant and Pee-Wee Herman)

At first the ear's infuriated! Then *Rush*—Geddy Lee!? Better—Robert Plant! Particles fun and balloons at the Fair behind the stands looking up and sucking in. *Hi, I'm Pee-Wee Herman—hee hee!*

How the Adam's Apple chortles this time of year! Bustle and hustle and sales and microchip bliss! Subway rides full of high-pitched squeals ain't only from the track screeching in and out of stations. It's a seagull world. "Oh and my boyfriend—well not really my boyfriend—but he said he almost lost my number and I was so running out of the clothing store and he called to say—hello? ... hello ... Jenny? ... hello ...—oh shit I thought I lost you—yeah—no I'm at—shit—Jenny?"

(Cough — Cough!) "I'm so frantic! I love you guys — that's awesome! Really?!" And then Keith Richards says: "That won't bust you! You gotta get higher than that though Roy (Orbison) had a way of gettin' up there in that pukka kind of way. No it ain't how come I fell off a tree!"

The compression of the larynx and the tightening of the nostrils. You can do it with a pinch between your thumb and forefinger or you can take in helium or inhale paint-thinner. They say the moon is loaded with it! **He** ... (reference great science journals).

And along the way on the streetcar a dude is going to the hospital and he's getting closer to where he has to get off but needs to touch base with home and on his cell phone and goes: "Hee, Hee, I think I'm getting closer ... ah ya mean I gotta come home 'cause I gotta get some balloons for da partee — hee hee!" And he kills you with the greatest phrase of surprise — "Holy Crackers!" his high-pitched squeal goes. Then he lets up and gets off and behind you four twenty-somethings from God-Knows-What-Neighbourhood start in with their own pitch and squeal — "My name is Andrew ... like Jeew ..." And his lady friend goes: "At least it ain't Tom Dick and *Hairy*! Like *Hairy*-dick! Oh LOL — imagine if they dropped the 'n' in the word Clinton (name of a street) and called it *Clitoris* Street!" And he repeats: "Like I'm not a Jeew. My name is Andrew. Like Jew. Which I know is a derogotree term but it's my name." And you feel the urge to turn and do, and ask: 'What is it that's derogat*ory* about the word 'Jew'?" And he goes: "Sorry. Sorry." And puts his hand on my shoulder and says: "I wanna explain. You see my name is Andrew and I know it's derogotree to say Jew but that's my name." "Your name is Jew?" I ask. And you can smell the thinner on his breath and he squeals as his girlfriend says: "You're a Jew. At least you're not Tom Dick and *Hairy*! Ha ha ha!"

And you say to yourself, the guy getting to the hospital had major Mensa advantage on these dudes. Maybe the thin Helium-like voice is how you have to pitch the vocal chords given the heavy bass rhythm of the rails and traffic beyond the car?

What was it with films from the 1930s? "Say, hey! You kids better get back to class — OHHHH!" Was it the sound equipment of the time that pitched the voices of most actors to a squeal-like tone? Maybe it was left over from radio days? The thinner and higher you spoke or sang, the clearer the voice was. Certainly, the discovery of the bass end of the sound spectrum and the use of equalizers were a God-awaited improvement.

And then visit a gym. Most of the guys with major pectoral and biceps muscles seem to have a thin high voice? Is it too much apical breathing or is it steroids? "Hee! Hee! Sure is hard to lift that weight! Hee! Hee!" He indeed. Why do men's voices heighten with weightlifting and women's voices deepen?

It's a seagull world and I don't mean Jonathan Livingston or Chekhov. Voices seem to be growing thinner in the din of contemporary post Valley-girl life.

HEE! HEE! HEE! Indeed! All those laughing gills and gulls whether we came from sky or sea in that high and ancient dinosaur age? And since we've touched on rock & roll, let's look or listen to a bit of Little Richard and The Bee Gees. The double 'ees' is already a hint. We're talking raw and honest rock & roll in its early days and the manufacture of smaltz from a band that once had a crack at musical integrity with *New York Mining Disaster* and *Massachusetts*. What happened to this brother band from Down Under? What's with the disco phase? Was Robert dating Gloria Gaynor or Frida Payne? Was that high-pitch squealed tone meant to get teenage girls to listen to it? Was Barry Gibb's silver lamé suit in the video release of *Stayin' Alive* an adventure in astro(naut) travel?

Of course in outer space it must be squeaky on the larynx so there's a chance, a very outside one, that the boys were meeting David Bowie's *Major Tom*. But "Ziggy Stardust", the Gibb brothers of the disco era, were not. Notice how deep Ziggy's voice is, in particular on *Space Oddity*. Notice also how the character Bowie created was developed from a great sense of real theatre, mime and even operatic gesturing. Notice how Ziggy Stardust was a creative force and the Gibbs were practicing the vulgarity of superficial market-driven entertainment a la Las Vegas. And stepping back to an earlier reference, how Little Richard's high squeals grew organically from the fury of momentum his rhythms necessitated.

I know you'd like to convince me that taste is taste and there's no accounting for it. And we all have our own but you can't tell me that, regardless of the great mega-sales, what the BGs were doing in these productions wasn't more akin to Dick Clark *Bopsicles* than, say, Alan Freed, and years later, Bill Graham. I do believe that helium sells. But maybe to the wrong people and it should stay in the hands of real astronauts and pop stars should get very little. But substance abuse has been with us since the beginning. It killed Elvis! Yet at least his lamé suit and vocal chords were gold. Is there a message in this? Yeah, there is. Listen to Al Jolson and if you need a high-pitched voice go for Brian Wilson. And if it makes you feel better, always understand we are all God's children, even if some of us sing from ball-squeezed *nasality*.

• • •

Then there was glue-sniffing Bobby LeMay standing on the lawyer's table in the juvenile courtroom and the HEE! HEE! HEE! coming out in rapid-fire succession like the funniest thing on earth was to be fourteen. And being caught for making Shirley MacKenzie pregnant at sixteen. Regardless of his auto-worker father and Bob Dylan's warning to not try "No Doze," Bobby got on board with the bullies, hoods and bikers in the neighbourhood and inhaled as much glue from his brother's airplane model kit as truancy allowed. He HEE HEE HEE'd his way through summer camp, ring hockey, pickup basketball and football on gravel, yet was most polite and dressed in his little grey suit and red tie every Sunday as he approached the altar for communion. It didn't help that in the back pews the boyhood dudes were sniffing large quantities of the latest mix, or had, just an hour before Mass. Parents always sat in the front. Kids and hoods in the back. And the moment the Reverend of the day would begin his sermon, the HEE HEE HEE's became most audible.

One particular Sunday Bobby decided to try Acid and see how far the light would go. "Holy shit! HEE HEE HEE!," Bobby let out, pointing at the rising stained-glass Christ over the Sanctuary. "Look at the @#%$-ing Light!" Bobby howled and yelped and stood up on his pew. The HEE HEE HEEs were picked up by the boys in the back. "Shit, look at Bobby! He's @#%$-ing blasted! Look at his Dad! Look at his Dad! His Dad's gonna kill him!" Startled by Bobby's outburst, Father Louis turned to view the wonder of Christ ascending. Soon, the girls throughout the congregation started giggling under their mothers' hat-brims.

Nobody noticed drunk Archie MacDonald who was usually the victim of incessant gossip and staring each week. Archie smiled silently, happy to see the spectacle unveil like the end of Days of Lent when the purple velvet robes were pulled from the marble statues. As he sat watching Bobby he thought of Sandy Lavoie, the French call-girl he would often visit on Saturday nights. "Yeah, I love that sorta purple...," Archie mumbled to himself. "... Hmm, that velvet purple like that dress....," he thought to himself—"HEE HEE HEE! I wonder...," Archie said in the confounds of his substantial inebriation, "... is it time yet to have those *Holy Crackers*?" And he rubbed his belly with gentle intent.

So from rock & roll to the gods we see ascending to the women we dream of, there is always assistance from beyond the corporal cage of bones (to half-quote Hamlet in his Shakespeare).

Bobby? He only made it to eighteen. I don't know if he went out laughing but he left a lot of it. The Church had the final word. But we, his friends — we have the laughs and tears. And still I can't hear a Bee Gees song without thinking of the kid in the white shoes who falls off the bridge when trying to impress his pals in *Saturday Night Fever*. Regardless of my love for country-rock (the counterpoint to the disco era), some of us did manage "Stayin' Alive."

DUDE STOPPING BULLFIGHTS

He ain't Spanish. That's all I know. He's a rugby player from England by way of New Zealand by way of Switzerland and he's polite as Roger Federer. You know, not like John McEnroe kicking the tennis establishment in the teeth. Mr. Diplomacy in action — "Ah c'mon ref! — are you blind?!" But the ref ain't blind. He's Dutch by way of The Virgin Islands by way of The Falklands. And he fought a war against the Argentines as a mercenary but was awarded a Star of Honour for his capture of Latin-blooded soldiers which remind him of when his father (and his grandfather) killed some *I-talyuns* in big WW2.

No this guy stopping bullfights ain't Spanish. He hardly even speaks the language. But his girlfriend does. She's been spending the better part of her life running away from the paella and moustached men in dark clothes. Didn't mind Mexico so much because there she felt superior in that colonial way. The way her daddy did when he said: "The Mexicans don't pronounce things like us. They are part Indian. Not pure-blooded like us!" Nobody as full of it as the denier of their background in their concept of identity. And of those there are many. Yes, it is nasty to put a bull through the torture of meeting picadors and then the master torero but should not one clean his own house before cleaning others? For the answer to this we go to one Donald Rumsfeld. He of the quote: "... the absence of evidence is not the evidence of absence."

So why stop the bullfights? Why does a non-Spaniard want to stop a bullfight? Is it really a bullfight he wants to stop or is it about his love for a young señorita he met years ago who gave him the oomph to want to be something? And she told him she would leave him if he didn't amount to something and he couldn't let her go?

So she had a plan. She would help him with his Spanish and introduce him to people she knew back home. Having worked as a spy, she knew her way around. Knew how to use others' talents or evoke their emotions for her purposes. Lloyd was perfect. A perfect find for her. So how could she get this simple Englishman to do her work? Bring down the bullfighting establishment? But at a certain point everything became very plodding. Like horses stuck in the mud. And he and she, an old cart that even oxen had abandoned. Someone else had to take over the narrative and that someone else could have been anybody (as e.e. cummings once said).

Yet, as the story goes, let's pretend for a moment *you were asked to turn off your TV and finish this story.* You are surprised. You say: *Why me? How could I write such a story given that I don't even write except emails and go online to buy the latest garden accessories?* A voice tells you you can do it though. Even if the last time you had anything to do with writing was on how to write greeting cards with references to flowers and sunshine and little bunny rabbits. In fact, at the time you were asked to sit on a locals arts jury to determine the winner of a writing prize. You were best friends with the donor of the award and did little theatre pieces for old folks and children. And, most importantly, you had been to Spain to see a bullfight!

Yes, you were there when the bull got stuck with the final puncture of the vein. You had gone because you loved Spain and its wine and dark-skinned men. The great Latin lovers of the screen like Ricardo Montalban and Desi Arnaz. To you, it didn't matter that Desi was from Cuba and Ricardo from Mexico. They were from the same place. The heat of your desire. The deep desire to run away from your middle-class husband and his suffering day-in day-out life as an accountant with an international client base. Through him though you were able to get a discount on your flight and accommodations. And so, the day you arrived you walked the streets of downtown Madrid in awe and held on to your purse for you had always been told that there were pickpockets and thieves at every corner. So you wore a disguise. You put on a black Cordova hat and found a red cape. Pulled out your long black leather autumn boots and hung a pink scarf around your neck just high enough to cover your mouth and lips.

As you conjured up the calm it took to be so far away from your suburban North American home, you worked so many details with your eyes that you began to get dizzy, and in the first block you walked, you fainted. This was not your plan but it worked out well in the end because a gentleman in white found you splayed on the sidewalk and brought you a glass of water, then carried you to a cab and to a local hospital. As you recovered that evening he came around to visit your hotel with tickets to the next day's bullfight. You were flattered and happy to go but the gore was too much for you and again, you fainted. The gentleman in white, Rodriguez, found himself taking you to the hospital once more.

Is this how I am going to spend my Spanish vacation?, you wondered as you lay in the hospital bed.

On a chair in the corner hung your disguise from the night before. You chose to wear those clothes to the bullfight and now you looked at them as though they were a curse. You remembered the Magic Show Evening at your son's local high school and laughed thinking how he ended up enrolling in Engineering at university. He continued to do magic tricks on weekends and the skill with which he moved his fingers over cards and flowers and rabbits and hats without a wand was exceptional. Greatness was not something you thought of or wished for your son. He chose security and you concurred. His father though wanted him to study acting and performance. Having been limited to the tedium of accounting, he projected his hopes for something more dynamic and vital for his son.

This was the part of your life known to some. The days of your disguise were known to none. The bullfights never happened and neither did you ever visit Spain. The writer needed a way out and you were working on a farm that summer. You never had a son and you almost had a husband and you were reading a travel book on Spain in the farm owner's small kitchen library. He had never been to Spain either but did have to stop a bull fight once when he brought in a new cow two farm bulls took a shine to. You were looking out your window and the farmer seemed to fall over holding his chest as he tried to scare the bulls off each other. You put on your alpaca poncho and ran out to see what had occurred and in the process frightened the bulls off into their own sections of the field. Then you called the hospital and, as you waited for the farm owner to recover, watched a story on public television about the great matadors of Spain. The narrator said at program's end that bullfighting was a dying art. You didn't believe that but, as you turned the TV off, you thought how really dreamy and good looking matadors were.

EDITORS

*(When you don't want to
get something done,
ask someone's opinion.)*

That's not always the case. But in most instances editors are writers themselves or critics who aspired once to be writers and assumed their comfort in "assisting" in the creation of other writers' works. There are editors like someone you know and trust maybe like a brother or a sister or even lover. Then there are those who work in the "profession" be it fiction, poetry or other. There are newspaper editors too.

The greatest experience a writer can have with an editor is having one who doesn't get in your way or helps open the way to your vision. A writer doesn't always know where he or she is going with their work and most like it that way to a certain point. I've had editors that want to change key aspects to a work that suggest I should write a whole other book than the one I may be working on at a given time. This advice comes often from a "marketing" perspective. I.e.: "Nobody buys poetry or fiction or non-fiction like that (meaning mine). You should write a memoir that has some family dysfunction or crisis in it — or at least be famous like Keith Richards or Elizabeth Taylor or someone who has lived a life most would recognize."

This of course flies in the face of quality of work and literary breakthroughs in style and aesthetics. This of course doesn't suggest that all editors aren't looking for quality to sell. It does however say that the editor or publisher via the editor has some substantial control on what is deemed marketable. Some come out with that clearly. Others can get up on the wrong side of the bed in the morning and in their disgruntled-ness or lack of understanding of the writer's stylistics, put their two cents and tastes ahead of what the writer is saying or trying to say.

You might think: *Well, that's the way the market is. Or editors are so* — *Suck it up!* Sucking it up or the suggestion that you live with the harness is half the point of this short piece. Sucking it up means "be tough" — grow thicker skin — let it go whenever someone doesn't do their job well — take the hard knocks that result — be insulted and turn the other cheek, etc. A point then about what I call loss of purpose, or dysfunction by "attrition", or default. Attrition in this case is when you don't hear back from a publisher or someone whose attention you are trying to get for your work. The publisher just doesn't respond. Some would even call this type of attrition "conflict resolution" but it is really "conflict avoidance" because editors "are too busy" to respond to work they can't bend to "their" liking. Some also call this "chickening out!"

Publishers have the means (power) to expose your work in the marketplace. And by marketplace I ain't talkin' bananas. I've heard one editor call this "the slow death technique." The idea behind it (or should I say method) is to correspond slightly to begin with then pull back. This establishes the power. All editors and publishers, record producers and media people in charge like to be pursued. The power lies in what people want from you. But if you are one of the above and don't want what an artist (in any of the mediums) has to give you, you do the slow death and let them gnarl in your non-responsiveness. The way to clear the decks on all this is to go independent.

I've sat with editors who want a certain kind of book. And I've sat with traditional record producers who want a certain kind of song. *Independence drives them nuts. They run when they hear the word 'cause there is nothing in it for them as in years ago, and most of all — there is no power they have over you.* This is something John Lennon had hoped to do with Apple Corps and Apple Records back in 1968. Some might have thought (and still do) that Lennon was naïve but he gained his power through Beatlemania and onwards, giving the corporate music giants at least a kick in the pants — ... *so an artist doesn't have to go into your office begging on their knees.* (my paraphrase).

This leaves editors and music moguls shaking at the bank as they are called both immoral and threatened with a shift to their comfort zones of controlling the purse strings. There isn't an artist (both great and small, highly talented and effective or weak in their expression, popular or outside on the margins), that has not faced the publisher, record producer, movie mogul *power of denial.*

With independence, the artist at least sits on the scales and swings balance into the equation. Yet the balance can tip too much towards independence where quality of work has no measurement or standard to go by. This is strictly from an aesthetic point of reference, which in the end however does affect marketability, subject to producers' and editors' determination.

There are very few editors who smile a lot or even a bit, and even fewer record producers who do unless they are getting an award at a corporate or association ceremony. Well, record producers do smile a bit more and often these smiles have to do with imbibing or some kind of "make me happy substance." Then they say #@$% a lot and thank all their pals and talk about how it could have been the end of the road if they hadn't worked and fought it out grind on grind. You know somewhere someone still had to cough up the money.

Take Clive Davis when Whitney Houston died. He was all over the podium at the Grammy Awards letting the world know he was there talking with Whitney day-in-day-out about her drug issues and great voice. He had to let everyone know he was pals with a beautiful young black woman like Uncle Clive but he sounded more like having to talk about his own struggles. Book editors aren't quite as gross and vulgar. They tend to mumble into microphones at ceremonies. And mostly 'cause they don't know how to speak into one.

But to be fair, let's not leave here without talking about the skills it takes to be a good book editor or record producer. A good editor can catch you when you are straying from your focus and can guess how a reader is going to go with or abandon your words. A good record producer has to find you a good engineer and set of musicians that bring your tunes to life. MAKE THEM LISTENABLE. The issue though is always taste. Again some Lennon. Sure, someone can make a Justin Bieber sound good but is that the same as someone making John Lennon or Eddie Vedder sound good?

When one thinks of this on balance, one similarity is that both Justin B. and Lennon became very popular and made loads of money for themselves and others. When we think of the differences, the argument becomes more substantial. One, Lennon, became a musician's musician and singer-songwriter through both need and the refinement of his raw talent. Listening to the origins of rock & roll and growing into the voice of both the avant-garde and of world peace. Bieber cannot be identified in this manner. Nowhere is there a hint that Bieber will become innovative in the studio, challenging the best record producers to change the medium. Nowhere will Bieber turn a phrase in song lyric that challenges the very foundation of song form and content.

To be kind, here's another similarity. Young teenage girls went mad to hear and see them in their different times. Here though is another difference. Lennon worked with three Liverpudlian friends to throw creative ideas off of and be influenced by. Bieber, though seemingly exposed to us in the mediums of iTunes and TV and even concerts of sorts, is more akin to Dick Clark's idol-making of the '50s and early '60s when Clark raided South Philadelphia's Italian immigrant community for good looking young guys who sometimes could and sometimes couldn't sing. Not a lot of talent musically. Squirmy for young girls. Tedious musical repetition. Superficiality. Vain for no apparent reason. In short—fabricated.

You might ask what this has to do with record producers or book editors? And, claim rightly, that Lennon was as vain and arrogant as they come. And understand the greatest difference is just plain talent and drive in Lennon, with the added ability to turn his celebrity into a cause for greater good. And sheer vanity in Bieber glowing from every medium possible.

What does this have to do with book editors and record producers? Two things are of note: 1) market and 2) taste. Marketability is more predictable than taste. Editors and producers are involved in both. Which force is greater? The ability and structure to sell or the taste of the audience? And can one influence the other? Market determines taste in the Justin Bieber case. In Lennon's though, while it could be argued that putting on jackets and neat haircuts affected taste, there was a refusal at a certain point to continue the masquerade and the hint was that the music was good. Real. Original and substantial with failures and successes.

The artist (Lennon) wanted us to know that it was a masquerade and even went so far as to condemn his and his band's prior work in order to break through to new artistic ground. Record producers (i.e. George Martin and Capitol Records) had to go with it as Lennon and his friends earned the freedom from their earlier period. Because of that phenomenon, attempts to re-invent that scenario were pursued by millions of wannabe artists. More importantly, many record producers and Artist and Repertoire representatives have since tried to recreate the scenario.

Is the difference the depth of talent between Lennon and Bieber? I don't know anyone who would argue that Bieber has the talent of a Lennon. The question is: Why do as many people, if not more, know of Justin Bieber than John Lennon? MARKET DRIVEN IDOL-MAKING. And independence propped up when in reality it is a method through which to gain attention (fame) and laugh all the way to the bank (fortune).

OSTRICH

She walks into the gallery tall and slender with a face that would attract the brushes of Modigliani or Michelangelo. She throws a slow soft smile your way, suggesting that she is into talking with you but not in a crowd. You tilt your head, signalling — *Let's talk outside.* She nods with a yes in her eyes.

So begins a movement of attraction and possibility. You meet her outside and arrange to call her. She has invited you to see her gallery and you are enthusiastic even though the night you visit it is a dreary November evening, raining and blustery as you try to straighten your umbrella to the gusts. As you enter the gallery space her sister greets you with a look of mild wonder. You look enough like someone else to her. The lady you have come to see takes you by the arm and walks you through an assortment of contemporary abstract art and the not unusual frames of landscape paintings by local and lesser known artists. You are not impressed yet you don't show it. What impresses you is your hostess' beauty. Her smile and movement is more alive than a thousand repetitive landscape frames.

But you get the feeling she would love it if you purchased one. You suggest a cup of coffee. She seems gracious yet pained. She tells you of her father who is not doing well and in the spaces left you mention you lost yours a few months before. She tells you you remind her of hers. You can't help but think of Freud. You know, every man is looking for his mother and every woman is looking for her father. But she is close to your age and you wonder if Freud's dictum still fits? She touches your arm and as the night goes on and comes to a close she tells you she's had fun. You agree to call her again and see a film at a local rep theatre. A week passes and you ask her how things are going when you meet for the movie. "It's the economy. Nobody's buying and everyone is careful with their money."

You soon realize you are a diversion from her strife. That what this woman wants is security and financing. She wants to meet people who will buy and support her paintings and her gallery. For this, you buy her a ticket and a membership to the film and theatre. You've even bought her popcorn and a meal later. She seems to be suffering and all you can offer is conversation and a late night kiss. Somewhere in her pain a smugness seems to exist. She tells you she is vital and her ex was not. She is tentative about the kiss. On the basis of your first encounter you miss the point of your second but call her again and detect a decline in her enthusiasm. Here is where you think of ostriches. The moment when the head goes into the ground. Where the possibility of love, let alone passion and romance, becomes reclusive. You wish that when her head goes into the sand she finds an egg of gold or whatever it is that ostriches find when they do that.

   She is tall and slender and informs you that her back hurts. You notice the bit of weight around her mid-section, slight as it is as she moves her arms to hide it. Her head starts dipping and you can feel it go downwards as you eat the last part of your meal. Whatever was or is in her that was or is attracted to a man fades in her fatigue. She wants to be cared for and may well be yet would be bored with the person who would care for her. You think to yourself a few days later that ostriches are beautiful. Their big eyes and long necks aside they hunt under the sand. You wish her luck as she disappears and consider what other animals you might meet that find you a more impassioned script or narrative. You touch wood and go on dreaming. You promise yourself to never stick your head in the sand. Whatever is to be found there?

MY EDITOR HAS A GOITER AND
WANTS TO EAT MY BOOK

Yes, well not the editor of this book. An editor at a publishing house who wants a book on dysfunction and pain and all those nasty things that her press says readers love to ingest. She has taken a bit of time to look at my manuscript and loves the writing yet believes it could be a series of short stories or essays placed in various journals. SNORE CANADIANA big time! Her job is to find material she can sell to her marketing people that in turn can sell it to a public weaned on New-Ageism and pseudo-psychology, self-help mass-market books.

She suggests memoir, which is kind of a cool idea but that's not what I'm writing. I understand supply and demand but I want to bring something different to the table. I want the reader to move from page to page without the tedium of psycho language and pretension of narrative. I don't want to have to turn every person I've every met into a motif or character to create my inner thoughts. I want the reader to enjoy language and determine meaning (if there is any) for themselves. I don't want to create sympathetic or evil, wicked characters. Nor do I wish to be known as an old fart writing the last pages of his life for a half-illiterate society. If she wants a memoir she will have to wait. Though there are many writers who would jump into this pool and believe their indulgence worthy of high literary honour.

The goiter. Well, I don't know how you get those but I think it's a thyroid thing. I remember this editor loved to drink red wine a lot. She couldn't get happy unless she did at least three glasses. Is that interesting? Not really unless I delve into why she seems to need more than a drink a day. She also says she wants to move to a small town. I could make an answer up as to why. But that again is a kind of snooping around. All I know is that she didn't have a goiter when I knew her years ago. How do you get one of those? Means you have to hide your throat and feel weight gain no matter how smart you are.

I guess I could write a short story *a la* Flannery O'Connor and title it "The Goiter in the Eves." That actually sounds more like Nathaniel Hawthorne? Or is that Nathanael West? Hmm? I think Hawthorne, and no less burdened. I could write it spooky and have the whole town peeking from behind trees in October air (around Halloween) as gossip grows and grows and as each person who gossips about the goiter they are peeking through the window to see, grows a goiter too. The whole town soon has people walking around with a variety of scarves to hide the growths. Now the question is what to gossip about besides the goiter? How about the editor sleeping with the town mayor who is married to a Vietnam-ese pole-dancer? They say a good book can be described in two sentences. That's like saying a reader wants to read blurbs and not a book. Now, back to my story ...

... so the dancer from Vietnam has three brothers who she has recently managed to have come over to join her in her New England town. This first lady of Smalltown (let's call it that for now) is quite the babe in the modern sense. She can't cook and has more pairs of shoes than Imelda Marcos. And on top of that she's been looking at pictures in a book about Amelia Earhart. When she has her first child she will call it Amelia. And if the child is male she will call it Kito. Well, Mrs. Mayor goes on to have Kito as her first born and we move the story on to have Kito flying a kite over the Boston river wondering why his uncles have not shown up. They were supposed to teach him all the manly things. Thing is, if they ever arrive, the manly things they have knowledge of would be worthless in Smalltown. So there sits Kito lamenting his plight and lonely as a kite in autumn ...

I take this beginning scenario to my editor with the goiter. She is surprised. She says: "I didn't know you were in Vietnam?" I say: "I wasn't!" She moves her scarf up. She coughs twice and breathes in deeply. She's loads of fun when she does this. I feel big words going around in her head but don't know what they are. Finally—she coughs it up: "I like creative non-fiction. There's a place for it in the market." "Then we will do that," I say, ordering her the finest red the restaurant has to offer. Goiter—get it?—waiter—red wine—order—get it.

SHE SAID: "I LIKE IT THAT LEONARDO PAINTS ..."

"I think he was a guy?" she says reflecting deeply on *The Mona Lisa.* "You know, in those days guys wore long frocks too. Leonardo probably painted himself at your age." This is another conversation at a gallery. We are actually viewing a Picasso exhibit but her mind keeps going back to Leonardo. "Just think of it for a minute." And I do. (I notice my gallery pal is fairly tall for a woman and somewhat slight-torsoed. Has a pretty face. Maybe if I put my glasses on I can detect some chin shadow?) "Well, I don't know. She (Mona Lisa) looks like some sort of nun who has found peace," I say. I wait for a response to see if my gallery pal's voice deepens in emotion and argument. "Gwad! She's a *he* at a younger age," she emotes with the voice I was expecting.

I turn quickly from the Picasso and get my reading glasses on. Finger on chin as if in a pensive mood, I glance over at her chin slightly and there it is — "five o'clock shadow"! "Do you think Leonardo had to shave at a young age if he was doing a self-portrait like you say? How about these Picassos? Do you think he's doing the same thing? He seemed to have a sense of humour with all those shapes and angles?" Covering her face with a cough she half squeaks to thin her voice and says: "I think he really didn't like women. That's why all the figures are distorted." "Hmm?" I respond.

Flashback . . .

This gallery pal was standing in front of one of the Picassos and I said excuse me as I tried to see the details in the painting. That's where our conversation started up. She had long blonde hair and wore floor-length black with shiny boots. Hair held back with a black Nike headband. I noticed first thing how big her hands were. And the dark-wine nail polish. She didn't move when I asked but turned her fairly wide shoulders away from my voice. Then she said: "Leonardo was a trickster. A magician. An alchemist with paint and inventiveness." I said: "What's Leonardo got to do with Picasso? I'm not following what you are saying?" "Just think of it," she said. "All those fine artists were living with suppressed sexual desire." "Geez, I don't know. I guess they painted some pretty randy stuff over the centuries," I offered. "By randy you mean men hungry for women, I suppose." "Well, yeah. It was guys and babes," I respond and inform with a bit of a smile. She takes what I say as an affront. Says again that Leonardo painted good. By good, I gather she means to her pleasing as there is no aesthetic consideration in her words. This is not the first "woman" I have met that has some heavy "Y" or "X" chromos happening. She moves most slowly into corners where men are. In fact, she makes a point of it. Moves her shoulders like a linebacker scanning an offense.

So, as she stares down Picasso's distortions of females and his loves, I think to myself that maybe, just maybe, Leonardo did some transgender shuffles. Why not? Who would know if he didn't paint himself in a younger year and called it Mona Lisa? Sure, there might be history saying she was this and she was that but we don't have a photograph and I don't think he ever wrote about it. Question I have is why this painting has sustained a reputation as one of his greatest works? There is something about Art History and then again something about Historical Fiction interpreting History. The latter seems some kind of desperate desire in our culture to connect with the past almost like going the route of adapting Eastern Incarnation practices and beliefs. Yet if history is this flexible why not say Mona is a guy in drag?

Someone will surely feel included in the movement of the centuries if that's the case. Even if it isn't, the same people will feel included in the re-arrangement of hard history. What is the need in our culture to make history fiction? What is the result of this re-assignment? The need? Vanity for many a writer and artist indeed. Other than that, a need to maintain a sense of questioning, though this might not be a conscious intent. The result? Confusion certainly. And entertainment on the level of reality TV shows. A lot of half-baked theories and books about ancient alien visits to our planet. And of course, interesting conversation with your next art gallery pal.

JOE KAPP, ANGELO MOSCA AND ZINEDINE ZIDANE

I n Canada in late November, the annual Grey Cup football week is held. One year, the organizers thought it would be a blast to bring together two old foes, now in their seventies, to make up over an incident where defensive lineman Angelo Mosca piled on a vital half-back and knocked him out of the game. The opposing quarterback of that game, Joe Kapp, fumed at the time in 1965, and fumed about it ever since in spite of a pretty decent National Football League career with the Minnesota Vikings.

There they were on Canadian TV sports channel TSN. At a certain point in the proceedings, Kapp offered Mosca a plastic rose as an olive branch and then called him a Son-of-a-@#@## or something to that effect. Mosca, seated with a cane he now uses for walking, swipes at Kapp and Kapp, full-standing, sucker punches Mosca as they scuffle in front of the live, laughing, yet somewhat shocked TV press crowd. It is always cool to see old guys go at it. In fact, Mosca had a career in Pro Wrestling (if you can call that kind of wrestling "professional").

How did these two arch-enemies get invited in the first place? They certainly had enough testosterone to still give it up so many years after the fact. The memory part was impressive. Like two tigers on each others' turf. A vendetta of sorts. Even the American networks picked the story up in sound-byte images. Not for its sport but for its oddity. As if old men fighting was unique to the YouTube generation.

Kapp and Mosca will never be representatives for dementia and Alzheimer's associations. Their previous performances in TV commercials, whether great or poor (both are Hall of Famers), will never supersede this most recent altercation. The popularity of it. People who don't even know Canadian football will remember only two old scrappers, ready to blow each other off the stage. Accidental Reality TV (as many ceremonies are shot live). But the same mindset that created these new programs allows for the celebration of male violence even in old age. Sports, because most coverage is live, is REAL TV.

Take the World Cup of 2006. Italy versus France in the final. Not an exciting game on the field by any stretch. Italy versus Germany in the semi-final being the showcase game. Yet part way into the final, one of the greatest players to come out of French football, Zinedine Zidane, presented viewers with something exceptionally different. This captain of captains in what would be his last World Cup appearance took insult from the words of Italian player Marco Materazzi who had taunted him all game long. In a fluster of rage Zidane, the coolest of geometric midfielders, turned and head-butted Materazzi in the chest. The card held up by the official was so RED that the Italian diaspora around the world claimed victim-hood to the nth degree. "How could he? We have been abused! ... etc., etc. ..."

Much is said on the field of play. Insults, taunts, racial slurs, even trips and violations by cunning athletes who attempt to do this out of the sight of officials. Yet with contemporary technology there are now three eyes: 1) The referee and linesmen working with him; 2) the stadium fans; and 3) the TV cameras broadcasting all over the world. (Note that video replays to contest referee decisions on the field are not yet permitted by the FIFA governing body). One could suggest that Zidane could have been more cautious about retribution for Materazzi's insults. He could have aimed the ball at M's head in the regular course of play. He could have clipped him off on a non-evident section of the field out of view of cameras and refs and officials.

But no. To the pleasure of many, in total rage and spontaneity, he threw his full head into M's chest. One had the feeling that, as Zidane threw his head forward, he had no regret. Surely France missed him dearly down to ten men when moments earlier they held momentum. But in that moment Zidane's own pride and honour was bigger than his pride or honour for France.

These incidents, the Kapp/Mosca kerfuffle and Zidane's head-butt, give fans a drama of: *See, they are just like us! They aren't heroes!* But the Greek, Roman and gods from various theologies and myth-ologies had fallibilities and maybe this is where the falling of present day sports heroes makes sense the most. And though Zidane chose to display the head of a Minotaur for that half-second, his clarity was our pleasure as much as our shock. Yet more than anything, the highlight reel ratings went through the roof. We don't really mind foul play. Unless you are betting your house and family on a certain game. Then there is hell to pay a three-headed-dog.

ONE

There is the concept of "one" as individual and the concept of "one" as driven by megalomaniac corporate "oneness."

As I sit in my study working at this text I look around the room and think of what identifies a person. There is a set of antique woods, four guitars, many, many books and CDs, magazines, paintings, photographs on the walls, etc. In the kitchen, many plates and the assortment of cutlery. And I think of repetition. And "ownership." Then I throw my thought down the street to the main thoroughfare and think of the number of restaurants, convenience stores, ice-cream parlours, *et al.* I think of the numerous articles of clothing, shoes, boots, socks.

Again, I think of ownership. I think of how identity is affected by what we own. Then I turn my mind to TV stations, the satellite channels, the competing interests of large corporations to central-ize their advertising and marketing powers. Here, the concept of individual "one" begins to dissipate, fade out, get lost in a blur of everything-ness. And then the internet with its millions upon mil-lions of appearances of one, one, one, claiming individuality yet delivering ad nauseam a drive of competitiveness for the best choice for "one's" attention.

So I choose to cut all down. One chair, one guitar, one pair of pants, one shirt etc. I don't have any animals so I have no need to apologize to Noah. Speaking of which, what do we do with all the gods? From Mercury to Allah to Christ to Buddha and Zeus, Xochiquetzal and all in between? Everything becomes one and one is everything, right? I've heard that said but how does it really happen? Do I stop counting after the first number? It is easier to say: "I only want one egg." But how do you deal with the fact there is more than one egg to have? Discipline? Fasting? Excluding? Focus? Denial? What does searching for "one" mean? What would drive that? Congestion. Too many choices. Someone's insistence that there is a sense of "other" than which you choose?

If we had one eye, we would be a Cyclops and that's been done in mythologies past and bad B movies. There is no way to have "one," be it an egg or star in the sky. But to sell the concept of "one" aggressively seems a violation of slowness and the sanctity of intimate relationship to objects desired or needed. This mild law the corporate world mocks yet wishes control over. From the legalities of logos to fear of lost identity one motivates most exchanges from the secular to the deeply spiritual.

The Protestants believe that you should have a one on one conversation with Christ/God. Catholics on the other hand adore a union, except in the confessional. Pantheists and naturalists believe there is an ecology that harmonizes all into a holistic "one" or dharma. Does this idea of "one" have to do with momentum, keeping us from ennui and the great inescapable and existential sense of inertia that life offers at its most solitary density?

Is it this "loneliness" that the corporations and sellers of near anything exploit in conscious and unconscious ways? The idea of corporation as religion is not a new one but it does seem to be on the rise. Dedication to a "brand" or philosophies of business practice. Belief in product and its "saviour" like qualities. Amazing sleight-of-hand and mind. An abundance of cleverness disguised as wisdom. A high degree of vulgarity unless you pay more and return to a concept of exclusivity. An illusion of being special or "one" of the few. Move from corporation speak to military for a half second.

The idea of one is huge though there may be chains of command. Even the concept or reality, if you like, of a bomb that can obliterate the planet though many can do it. And the idea of "one better" comes into the frame. "We now have a bigger and better and more effective bomb." Is a bomb to be considered like a deodorant? That would sure take care of all the under-arm odour and clean away body hair for sure.

ROY ORBISON

Zimmerman Bob once said something to the effect that Roy Orbison, 1960s country and pop star, had a voice like an opera singer. If we take Zimmerman's allusion to heart we see and hear a voice that uses octave dynamics unlike other singers of his genre. But the deeper aspect of his songs and voice (whether Z intended this or not in his comment) is the drama of emotion, the repetition of themes: love lost, existential loneliness, the beauty of love just out of reach. Except perhaps in his first major hit *Pretty Woman* in which the woman for some unknown reason (but maybe his purr in an earlier verse) decides to return and answer his plea for her company. Is this opera in its own way? I had the opportunity to feel this out first hand when a few years back I was commissioned by a local opera company to write a libretto for a fifteen minute opera.

As I sat with director, composer and singers, I was first struck with how collegial all participants were. There was an aspect of fraternity, sorority and downright high school cliquishness to the endeavour and mood. Given this was not a full length opera and a couple of us were novices to the form, the in-knowing aspects of the company were distinct. The artistic director and company founder waved his baton like a British school master and was flattered when I called him "Good Master Dywane." He ruled his roost.

Brought in an a stage director who had read my script/libretto a month or so beforehand and had nothing good to say about it. His claim to expertise was having sat on a North American Opera panel and having produced other "shows" across the continent. So if two people can form a cabal, these two managed it, including their administrators. The stage director's comment on my text was that there was not enough language that allowed for operatic movement. That the work was slight and had to be re-written to suit the needs of operatic performance.

The text I had written was about two women meeting at a Salvador Dali exhibit somewhere in a mid-Atlantic city. The subtext included a storyline about their cheating husbands. My intent was to challenge the manner in which art is perceived and the pretensions involved in the process for the two characters and any like them across the arts. And to underline the pains of truth (their cheating husbands) that existed for them and the dynamic that comes to light when the suppression of unhappiness meets absurdity and surrealist expression. When I wrote the stage director back I underlined the above and his response was something akin to "My God! I didn't see that. Yes! Yes, that's amazing!" And with that I was hired on with enthusiasm.

Each morning before I arrived for rehearsal I would sit with my guitar and play out a few of my favourite songs. And some of my own, composed during the last half year. I did this as I was on schedule to record an album of original pieces and also to get myself away from the heavy focus of the text I had written and how to improve it some before the *singers* got a hold of it. I italicize singers because they were also required to be actors. Around the same time my sister had mailed me a collection of Roy Orbison's greatest hits for my birthday and I loved putting it on to just get my mind in a freer place and enjoy great pop songs of old.

As for the text I was writing, I had been interested in Brecht's theatrical writings—and the Theatre of the Absurd and surrealist literature—and wondered how I could write a text that couldn't be ruined regardless of bends and twists adaptation of my words could bring from composer to stage director to singers. So as I would step away from the desk and make a good cup of espresso, I would listen to Roy and how he seemed to do it all so easily. The voice lilting just at the right moment and the great guitar grooves that moved around his vocal. It reminded me of drama. How drama could be created in three minutes. How to translate that into text you only had fifteen minutes for. (Longer than a pop song yet shorter than a theatre piece.) And I thought about the aforementioned words of Bobby Z in a recent issue of *Rolling Stone Magazine*. There I was, trying to fuse all this together for the perceptive eyes of opera audiences.

The composer was insistent that we begin our session (we met separately a few times before full cast) with a bottle of wine. This could be four in the afternoon. Seven at night or most intriguingly, at nine in the morning. Always a drink needed to begin his scoring to my text and words.

My idea was that he write something jazzy and bluesy to fit the aura of a contemporary art show. Something hip-sounding and on the cool side. A way of setting up the tension in the subtext. You know, everybody knowing and smug and at ease with their sense of themselves—but underneath it all these women are close to ruin in spirit and mind. What better way to take perception to another level than introducing Dali and his painting "The Temptation of Saint Anthony." In this work, Dali has elephants on stilt-like legs and St. Anthony is holding back temptation. To me, the temptation was to see things differently. I believe that is what Dali is saying through biblical metaphor. Not so much the traditional temptation of the Saint, but the temptation for viewers of the work to see things from another perspective.

So Roy Orbison was a simple balance to this pretty heady stuff. And of course because I had a composer who needed to drink more than compose, or needed to drink to compose, I loved the Roy moments before sessions began. And the simplicity of his effect stayed with me day in and day out. As we sat in rehearsal I watched the singers hit their notes and get in tempo and mood. The gap was in performance of character. One woman was written as a sophisticated lady with tiny binoculars for opera viewing strung around her neck that she used for gallery visits. She was the older of the two and had befriended the other woman at a social gathering. Yet the woman she invited was what you would call a "soccer mom" and when she visited the gallery she wore field binoculars. The kind you would bird-watch or attend sporting events with. The dichotomy in the two characters would show and allow the variations in perception and grow into the absurd nature of the text so as to allow the power and reality of the subtext to have substantial effect. I.e.: one could laugh at the absurdity of their perceptions and on the other hand, empathize with the truth of their confusion and heartbreak due to their husbands' philanderings.

Roy for me was the key to getting away from the bad performances and drunken composer. He was simple and emotive yet had the capacity to express joy even in his aloneness. And though Bobby Z's comment on Roy's operatic possibilities were somewhat over enthusiastic, I took the lighter part of Z's rating and enjoyed the lilt and tone. Roy was never an opera singer and likely never could become or want to be one. Octave range is not enough. However, there is something about opera performers that hit all the right notes but can't act their way out of a paper bag. You can hide this with costumes and sets and lights and good hors d'oeuvres but a bad actor is a bad actor whether in tights carrying Viking swords or any of the accoutrements the stage director deems necessary to move plot along. Rarely is a character in opera developed from the text inward.

This is the antithesis of The Method of Stanislavsky or its Americanization by Lee Strasberg's Actors' Studio. Opera acting seems more a vehicle for the voice and the music and, if lucky, the narrative. Opera singers are trained to sing. They lack training in acting except for gesture though occasionally the charisma of a certain singer can galvanize with raw energy and deliver character along with great voice. But most opera stars are not as interesting as the sets and small parts players who play ghosts, kings, queens, devils, fairies and farmers.

In short, this is far from the nature of pop music and other forms where many performers have developed a keen sense of performance character. Notably Tom Waits moving through the underbelly of America and certainly Mr. Z with his many hats to match his various styles of writing and sometimes vocals. This is not to confuse two styles of music and performance but to underline that opera singers have a long way to go beyond gesture and superficial servitude to the music to engage an audience with any sense of character.

This is what I was confronting with the opera libretto I was asked to create. Tepid acting and schoolmarm-ery direction. Thank god Roy was there in the morning. When I finally went to opening night the audience seemed to enjoy the work. It reminded me that all these works start with words and thoughts. The arts of acting and singing come later or in some cases (certainly this one) don't come at all. But audiences can be polite. One reason being that when performance ends it is a relief to get up from those staunchy seats and race off to the bar.

This is where I always found my composer associate. Happily singing my praises as long as his glass was full. To him, opera was not only a chance to create but an opportunity to see what wine was being served. And so, no, Roy Orbison ain't no opera singer but damn! — he's good at what he does and I will never have to work with him to find out if the devil had him in the drink and helped his material happen or not. I suppose there's a touch of judgment in all this. But whoever claims not to use judgment is more than slightly hypocritical and spends a lot of time doing nothing but sitting on a fence, being polite and praying for things to fall into their laps or onto their tuxedo lapels.

LATE FOR THE SKY

(Billy Joel's *The Stranger* versus Travis Bickle)

The heyday of American Realist film was the 1970s until mid-to three quarters decade and the arrival of the blockbuster, most saying it was Steven Spielberg's *Jaws* that killed the form. A bit earlier in the decade we had the beginning of Martin Scorsese while later into the decade radio played Billy Joel's *The Stranger*. This invited us to two new realities. One, the story of a crazed cab driver, ex-Vietnam vet who was out of place in big town New York (*Taxi Driver*). The other, a pop-ish attempt to appear hip and on top of everything from relationships to inner feelings to an over-view of the world around him.

Billy Joel however gave us *Piano Man* in 1973. His one man piano and long narration of a night over a microphone playing songs to folks in the torpor of their loneliness came on the back of Harry Chapin's long song *Taxi*. Two interesting perspectives from which to view life and create a song. Two fairly alone places in society. A piano man and a cab driver. As the decade moved along and success met Joel and Chapin faded into FM radio, a sense of realism seemed on the minds of many American film directors. However, this movement to realism for the most part began some years earlier with *Easy Rider*, Dennis Hopper's road movie about the counter-culture. The odd-man-out, the marginalized anti-hero began to reappear with all the force of a new generation of Method actors following in the footsteps of Brando, James Dean, Montgomery Clift and Rod Steiger.

In music we had disco as the latest phase yet there was also the rise of Gram Parsons' Flying Burrito Brothers, The Eagles and country-rock as a new pop form. The other force in popular music was the singer-songwriter. Besides Joel, who was somewhat unique because his main instrument was the piano, from California came Jackson Browne whose depth of expression rivalled Dylan Z from the previous decade. His mid-70s collection *Late for the Sky* travels the road from lost love to consideration and disenchantment and lament of the loss of the open-minded 60s. A practitioner of the long song, Browne was both political and capable of almost Mahler-like chords progressions and melodies. Lyrically his competition were Bruce Springsteen out of New Jersey and Tom Waits out of San Diego. But Browne's articulation of a generation lost after the exuberance of the open road stood on higher ground. His instrument was also the piano, and if one compares his songs to Joel's, the difference between pop-for-show and popular song as an art-form becomes apparent.

Billy Joel post-*Piano Man* wrote melodies and lyrics that sounded like perfume and hair advertisements. Sure, there was talk in his work about love and the society we live in but it was his treatment of those themes that showed his pop-ish-ness. Browne on the other hand, required you to stay in the pocket for an intelligent and emotional length of time. Closer to literary form or poetry than mere song. He had a sense of the troubadour in him. He was alienated. He was able to stand back from the actions of the heart and reflect with doubt and sorrow. It was not only his subject matter but his treatment of the subject matter. Where Joel was catchy, Browne required you to pay attention to complexity of feeling and perception. Joel had some of Frankie Valli and the Four Seasons in him.

Browne had a uniqueness that was difficult to compare even to previous and contemporary songwriters. His "voice" was both panoramic and intimate, able to speak of loss of innocence and resonate with the cultural mood of the time. Most striking and haunting on his *Late for the Sky* album was the title track: *How long have I been sleeping? / How long have I been running alone through the night / ... of the bed where we both lie / late for the sky*. This lyric is featured in Scorsese's *Taxi Driver*. The scene where Travis Bickle becomes more and more alienated and is viewed in his ratty apartment watching of all things *Dick Clark's American Bandstand*.

Travis is a few scenes away from an attempt to assassinate the presidential candidate. He is distorted in his loneliness and trying to make sense of things bigger than himself. Travis is the polar opposite to the smug male pain and tepid lament of Billy Joel's "stranger." This "stranger" is always in control, seeing situations that he has no real pain about. Bickle is a mess. He comes from small-town America to find something to survive for or merely just to survive. *The Stranger* sits on a bed (see album cover) and looks cutely at a mask of a supposed lover, or a reflection of himself. But you know there is not true suffering. It is pop at its most pretentious.

Bickle though is a study in the line of existential characters. More Tennessee Williams or Arthur Miller or Elia Kazan. He could easily be transposed into an Albert Camus play or novel. He is lost and subject to the fates that surround him. He cannot meet a balance within himself thus he distorts to become part of something. To belong. *The Stranger* (ironically one of Camus' most celebrated novels) is willing to eat at fine Italian restaurants and be hurt by kisses missed as if life was a high school prom. From *Piano Man* to *The Stranger* Billy Joel lost his power of poetry. He went from raconteur to light-weight "feeler of things." One can detect a sense of trying to find the right formula for a hit in Joel's post-*Piano Man* music and lyric.

Scorsese's Bickle is after a different kind of freedom. As is Browne's protagonist in *Late for the Sky*. One does not know how he will end up scene to scene or song to song. You cannot predict reactions nor actions to the world Bickle or Browne live in. The fates will align for them and they will interpret external forces as forces that give them direction or no direction at all. They try love but in Bickle's case he is immature and pornographic (in an innocent way) about love and intimacy. With Billy Joel's stranger you continue through each song to feel he is writing song, not experience. And, with Jackson Browne, you find that he is able to craft and experience at the same time at a very sophisticated and literate level. Literate in the manner of expressing emotion that is rarely acknowledged or articulated by male or female narrators and artists attempting to enter the music markets.

CELEBRITY JOURNALISTS

("Yellow Up!")

The editors of newspapers across North America seem to think we like to have pictures or sketches of the columnists and reporters covering everything from sports to business news and all in between. This projection of the-face-behind-the-story does little to improve or make worse the writing presented. There seems to be a sense of accreditation disguised as giving you a sense of familiarity. Everyone wants credit. I suppose that money you owe on your credit card ain't enough.

But honestly, why the photos and the sketches? So we can see their eyes and know they are telling the truth? Well, we all know how a story can be bent so let's not insult the truth here. Some photos and sketches make the writer look haggard and old. Some make the writer look like they just woke up. But is the story or column about the writer or the story? This is after all "journalism," no? I understand a photo of Tiger Woods grimacing if he lands in the bunker but do I need the reporter of the story smiling or frowning in static day to day repetition over him? Do these writers have so much doubt about their talents that they need to stick themselves to a story like certain produce distributors need to stick their little logos on an apple or banana? What is with the logos on a plum? You ever try to peel a logo off a plum so you can wash it and eat it for lunch? No chance. You peel the logo — you get a gash in the fruit and you have to eat it right away or you get fruit juice dripping in your lunch bag.

The other development *a la press* with the advance of technology is the blog and video of a writer or columnist on camera speaking to the issue they are covering. This becomes a bit more intriguing. You get another dimension. Get to see them move and that includes eyes, the shoulders, the hands, etc. Of course if they are good looking, you likely won't hear much of the story. If they are not good looking, you probably turn the video off. If they are in between, you listen at least and maybe not look. Then there's the blog. It isn't enough that these writers get paid hundreds of dollars a week to write their opinions or a short version of the truth and news, but they use the platform to say even more yet most blogs border on gossip. Now if a writer has talent and a sense of humour that's probably a good thing.

If you are looking for expertise you often don't find it. That, you find in the classifieds and the obits. Clear. Objective — this person died or this person was born or this couple got married or this person is advertising their apartment for rent or selling canoes or microwave ovens. The answer to all this is that the blog, the video and the photo and sketch, and more often than not the column — are market driven. They are supposed to help sell the paper and possibly the writers' other works when they are moonlighting writing plays, self-help books, essays for journals, birthday cards for friends and family. But the mother paper is the big winner or loser here. Since the mid-1990s most papers introduce their name in the course of a story—I.e.: *As the* _____ *reported last week with its ground-breaking investigation of* _____ . As if we live without memory and have to be reminded who did what when we are reading it in the self-same named paper.

This *braggadocio*, arrogance and vanity is prevalent in the competitive and congested broadcasting market. Take for example one WB who works for NNC (backwards). He seems to live on the balls of his tongue and reminds you as much as informs you of any news development that you are "watching the best news on the best news network on television ..." and that he'll be back in just a couple of minutes to tell you more of how the "best news network" will give you the "best news" and it's the best. For sure? He, as his network's on-air representative, is doing all he can to get you to stay tuned yet watch the network's sponsors' ads and be pulled by gravitational and magnetic force field to his network.

It is true that you have a choice and don't even have to turn on the television or internet for that matter but maybe you think since you pay a certain amount each month, maybe, just maybe there will be more quality news and less "me, me, us" selling to the whole idea of watching television news and getting relevant in-depth non-repetitive coverage of vital news throughout the day. And further, when you go to commercial break, every second item advertised is about the very station and program you are already watching. Usually with a pitch of visuals and sound bytes that try to gain your emotion viscerally and "in your head" simultaneously. In short, broadcasters throw everything in their realm at you, not even trusting the phenomenon of after-image, that what you see will stay with you anyways. This overdrive causes nothing less than intellectual congestion and fatigue. You actually feel relief turning the TV or internet off and you have paid for that relief in dollars and time and may have to pay even more for an aspirin.

Yellow journalism used to be the cheap news. The news of gossip tabloids and the news that wasn't "news." The gossipy aspect was looked down upon by the major papers and broadcasters and you took comfort in the fact and promise that the majors were not given to trite and superficial coverage of the private lives of celebrities and conspiracy theories about aliens landing in the back yard of nowhere Idaho or the front yard of the Queen of England. This cartoonish coverage was only done in the yellow press. Not the majors or "serious" papers. But things turned for the majors when the number of readers of yellow journalism began to soar in the mid to late '80s. The majors failed to see it coming but didn't hold back from getting on board eventually, regardless of the loss of integrity of broadcast and journalistic standards and qualities that kept press and broadcast journalism real and verifiable.

The underlying truth to the majors turning "yellower" was motivated by nothing less than the money that sell sell selling could bring in from advertisers and that a larger demographic net could be cast. Interestingly, the yellows didn't sell much advertising. What they sold was straight UN-adulterated trash. Poor writing and reporting for the masses and growing number of semi-literate North Americans turning more illiterate every day. As the age of the internet came along, the potential for readership and advertising revenue threw a curve at the printed press and major broadcasters. With the exception of PBS and the Canadian Broadcasting Company in Canada and Britain's BBC, every moment became one of potentially greater gain in advertising revenue yet not in intelligent un-biased reporting.

As the majors "yellowed up," the identity of the journalist became more vital at times (many times) than the story reported on. One recalls the news of John Kennedy's death here. Somewhere in Walter Cronkite a subtle, humble man (at least the persona presented on screen). There was humility and a voice that could stop a war from escalating. A calm and confidence with the soul of both experience and wonder. Like Edward R. Murrow before him, Cronkite's delivery of the news was straight up and relevant to the state of the world. Advertisers were few as stations were also few yet there seemed a decency, a line drawn between the vulgar and acceptable as to what was trite and where to put it and not to confuse it with news of vital importance.

The speed of news delivery became a point of import as well. From Murrow to Cronkite and up to WB on NNC (backwards), news began repeating itself quickly and became available at any hour of the day or night. The effect of this repetition was to dull the viewer's senses and what was sacrificed was in-depth steady dialogue or monologue in the traditional style of older news broadcasts. Advertising more and more determined the shaping of an hour of news. And in the guise or attempt to capture the wider and culturally diverse demographic more than old white males were presented as hosts, anchors and reporters of various news programs.

Diversity does not equate to a decline in quality yet it became evident that broadcasters and their sponsors knew that going after the cultural variations in society could help sell and increase ratings. Some of the new journalists and faces from various cultural and ethnic backgrounds were schooled in the strong news presentation and some were not. Some were only there for their cultural difference on the superficial level of their visual impact. Not for their perspective culturally or because they were African-American, Latino, Asian-American, etc.

The intent of this piece is not to go into in-depth analysis of media and the growth of yellow journalism as much as it is to say we give power to people. We give money to people (via our internet and TV cable fees) to interpret the world for us. To offer their expertise. And in many cases in contemporary broadcasts, social media and print mechanisms, we are being sold short. The colour of money has turned yellow and to which colour it turns from here is anybody's guess.

ASPHALT AND PLASTIC

Roland Barthes in his 1957 text *Mythologies* drew consideration to the semiotic relevance of plastic and its invention and use. His suggestion was that something beyond the confines of nature, something man-made, made us less dependent on nature for our everyday needs. His view on the proliferation of plastic was in part awe-struck. A peculiar position for a Marxist theoretician.

Barthes' short cultural essay always reminds me of the green and orange plastic chairs at our cafeteria back in university days. I believe there were other colours, like purple, yellow, event fuchsia, as the makers of these pieces of furniture were touching on the idea of making most common and public environments somewhat of a playground. Who can't remember "Lego" plastic blocks from their kindergarten class? I thought that, because our university college was named after the Irish patron Saint Patrick, our chairs were green and orange in some kind of contemporary homage.

As I attended classes in the evening, I worked days on a road construction crew paving everything from rural highways to parking lots to driveways. For anyone who has done that kind of work, the idea and concept of plastic is very foreign except for one distinct item. The hard-hat. And these hats came in a variety of colours. Some symbolized authority. That was the white hat. Others, blue, orange, green and red symbolized different trades. I.e.: electricians wore green, plumbers, blue. But the asphalt was black as bituminous coal. Sticky, hot and smooth.

What you never wanted was rain coming down with a full load in the paving spreader for the asphalt would congeal and cool into almost hard lava-like rock. Strangely enough, as I was studying Barthes at night in evening sociology classes, one of the main characters at work during the day was a dude named Rollie (Roland), the roller operator. Of course being naïve and given to inconsequential synchronicities (coincidences really) I noted that Barthes' first name was Roland like *Les Chanson de Roland* which I had studied a year previously in French Literature Class.

Rollie was French-Canadian. Roland Barthes studied and taught at the prestigious Sorbonne in Paris, France. Yet Rollie had the face of a Gallic warrior. Broken teeth and sharp chin with a tussle of light-brown locks underneath his red plastic hard-hat, each day he would stand like Charles de Gaulle atop his roller and declare more than question — *Rayhain tuddaye?!* His hope (and ours) that a great downpour would cool the humid air and shut down work before it began so we could go home and rest our hot tired bones. For working on a road crew is very much like military work. Just ask all the contractors that made a fortune in all the foreign wars building and re-building the infrastructure in the name of "progress." (For more on this see Marlon Brando in *The Ugly American.*)

The work crew bosses didn't like Rollie much. They would throw glances of contempt his way across the hot road given that the roar of machinery made the use of vocal chords useless and ineffective. But Rollie's *Rayhain tuddaye?!* could be heard clear and loud above the roar and din. Yes, the bosses wanted to get rid of Rollie but Rollie was a union man. And further to this, Rollie wanted his brother-in-law Nelson brought in to work on the crew. Now, Nelson was the polar opposite of Rollie. Quiet, focused, humble in his small town rural manner, he had the most fantastic name — Nelson Beauregard — which brought up images of great flurries of Confederate Civil War cavalries sweeping into battle waving their sabres. And because of Nelson's honest, substantial work ethic, Rollie benefitted in that way politics works on one of these crews. I.e.: You get rid of Rollie, you lose one of the best men to come along in a long time, who covers for others and begins and finishes every task with precision and can take the heat of order after order. And lives on raw hot-dogs and cola to boot!

That's right! Every morning when the canteen coffee truck came by with hot coffee and snacks for break, Nelson would buy raw hot-dogs and cola and whip three dogs down. In the age of health food and greater, healthier living, Nelson would consume these "little baloneys" (as he called them) and say to the Italians on the crew: "Want some? It's just like what they do on pizza." The more senior Italian men would recoil at the smell and suggestion of his offer. Their wives packed asparagus and egg sandwiches, plums and apples, cool cucumber salads and cold espresso which they kept well-temperatured in coolers. When lunch-time came these men would sit under a leafy tree to avoid the heat and make a work site lunch period resemble a Sunday picnic. And they insisted all machines be turned off, trying in some way to replicate the rural ease of the hometowns they came from.

Nelson and Rollie came from hard, harsh mill-towns along the Gatineau across the Ottawa River. They grew up with sulphur from paper mills and the exhaust from small manufacturing factories. One of these factories made plastics, including bags for supermarkets, umbrella handles and hardhats. As the season wore on there was little rain to be seen and with the hours long, a sense of camaraderie sustained us through the dust and oil and heat of pain. Then the long weekend leading up to Canadian Thanksgiving approached. So here we were, getting closer to a three-day rest and spanking true that morning, Rollie gets up on top of his machine and hollers — *Rayhain tuddaye?!* There were a few clouds in the northwest sky. His question held some promise, and if his prediction came true we would all have ourselves a four-day weekend.

Now, semiotics, the study of signs and significance of language and lexicography, is not something that you have dialogue about on a construction crew but as some thunder rolled in the approaching clouds, Rollie says: "Me Rollie, roll 'um thunder" in a Native rain dance cadence. I yelled up over the machine: "Rollie — is it going rain today?" And he started to stomp one foot down on top of the roller: "Rayhain tuddaye! Rayhain! Rayhain! Ray-hain!" In short order the clouds opened. He laughed and howled and we were informed that we would be packing up and heading home.

In his enthusiasm Rollie started the roller and moved it along the edge of the highway we had been working on. These highways often have fairly deep ditches and if you get too close to the edge you can go over. Rollie kept up his stomp and dance as he stood above his levers and grinned and yelped at the sky. His roller moved too close to the edge in his inattentiveness and over he went tumbling in the same direction as the fifteen ton Buffalo Springfield roller. We stood in shock as we saw the roller tumble and Rollie disappear under it.

Nelson flew to the site: "Rollie? Rollie?! Ya okaye?" The other men ran to the tumbled machine. The foreman cursed and told all of us to stand back and sent someone to his crew truck to call in the accident. Within minutes Rollie jumps up all smiles and yells: "RAY-HAIN TUDDAYE! Rayhain! Rayhain!" His fortune was that, when the roller tumbled, he fell into a small dip in the ditch which protected his body as the roller went over him. Missing him completely. The older men scolded him for his carelessness. In a language he had no way of understanding they told him he was a fool and idiot but he picked up the vibe and raised his left arm as he stood in the ditch and brought his right hand down quickly over his left bicep: "No speeka da Hingleesh! No spinache! Va Funnycoolio! Yahoo!"

So began my deeper study of plastics and asphalt as, with the end of the long weekend, I gave thanks and left the asphalt trade to continue my studies. Barthes would have loved it. He would have loved Rollie. Maybe not lunched with him and Nelson and his cold hot dogs but he might have said something akin to: *Semiotics eese sumtimes da wey teengs eese!*

Here's to you Rollie, the roller and Roland Barthes and *Les Chanson de Roland.*

PS: *Too much synchronicity can ruin your day. Not enough of it can make it hard work.*

SONGS FOR THINKIN' ABOUT

Woody Guthrie. The above title is attributed to the Jeffersonian wit of Woody's son, Arlo in a retrospective on Guthrie and Huddie Ledbetter (Leadbelly). "Songs for thinkin' about." Thinking about what? Thinking about girls? Thinking about death? Thinking about money and going to see the dentist when it cost too much? Thinking about movies? Thinking about the Bible? Allah? Christ? Buddha? Drive-in horror movies? Dichotomies and nuances in the translations of languages and dialects? Banana splits?

Though Guthrie senior may have enjoyed some of the above in his travelling, his focus on the marginalized and poor folk of the American Dust Bowl, and the politics that did little to get them out of their jam, has lived on through the music and words of

Bobby Z, John Mellencamp, Bruce Springsteen, and a slew of other protest voices whose work started in the good old USA and found export for itself around the globe.

A good friend recently asked me: "Where is the Woody Guthrie that is going to write the songs about the growing starvation and food shortages already in the world, especially in under-developed countries?" I point to "USA for Africa" and "Live Aid" propelled by Michael Jackson and Boomtown Rats frontman Bob Geldof in the 1980s. My friend says: "Yeah, but that was thirty years ago and it's getting worse. Geldof got a knighthood and Jackson's dead. What do you think John Lennon would be doing if he was still alive?" I answer that I think Lennon might be involved. But that's based on hindsight. I say more likely that he would not be prancing around the stage like Mick Jagger.

Yet beyond the tragedy of losing Lennon, the world is compressing at a rapid rate. Food shortages are real and even effecting areas of the globe known for high sustaining productivity. These questions my friend can't answer straight up. He can suggest what might be done or prepare in some manner for what he fears but the effects of his care are mostly conversational. I personally don't believe hordes will come and eat beavers and all the deer in the forest. I do believe aid will continue to flow into countries more in need. I suspect that, if a drought came and water level drops occur in middle Canada, it will remain verdant unless there is a great war that nukes all possibilities of survival. I think people like to be altruistic. Like to feel they are doing good. A lot of people do this without announcing it or making it a religion of sorts. I think of the songs of Guthrie and ask my friend why he needs any others? Aren't the many already written, recorded and available to all enough to have the point made?

His answer is that this must be a constant reminder. That just because we have a history of dustbowls and droughts it isn't just history. It can happen again. I agree that that is likely true. He wants me to change my opinion about his farm being raided though. He would still be displeased even if I did change my opinion and concur. I suspect there would be surprise if I changed my actions and recognized the little details that make up my life and injure the environment and ecology. I don't drive a car. He has two. He says it's a necessary evil. How else to get the food around and farm the farm without machinery? I smoke. Didn't for a number of years but started again. Not to annoy him. Not to annoy anyone. I ride a bike. I help out on the farm.

I understand Woody and Arlo and all the others that came and will come after them. I think here of my parents' existence in agrarian Southern Italy. More akin to how my farm friend seems to want to live. They suffered and persevered. He's transplanted to his farm from urbanity. I think my pal would like them. Maybe more than he likes my attitude and ways. They might have been able to teach each other something. Don't remember much philanthropic instinct in my folks. My mother had no issue with feeding hungry beggars who came to our later North American door. But she didn't preach it like an emergency—she just cooked enough to store for winter and go around. My farm pal is slightly impressed with this. He says I come from good blood but regardless of how well I can write a song, that I have a long way to go. That's rarely a motivator. I let his condescension and patronizing language pass over my head like a tired wind. I have a garden.

The philanthropy of western celebrities *has* been effective in bringing attention to the issues of political corruption and starvation *et al* but where is the song, the songwriter, the artist that can change the direction, pointing to future and imminent disaster? My friend believes that when the food runs out in the cities, if a disaster of huge proportions hits, the city dwellers will be running to his fields for food and sustenance. I wonder how true this scenario would be and imagine it for a moment. What would my friend do? Would he run for the hills at the millions approaching? Would he say: "Well, me and Annie, we had a good run of it for twenty-five years and now it's time to share"? Would he preserve what he has created and give it up with grace until his end? Would he alert all his farming community friends and stand up with rifles in some bizarre Alamo moment?

The answer to what he would do, what I would do, how it would all play out is very different in speculative conversation than what it might really look like. That's the catch. You can talk about it all you want but what would you do? Help 'til you drop or fight 'til you die? How to prepare for the incursion?

My friend doesn't really have any answer to that yet I get the sense that at least his friends and family would be taken care of for as long as possible. He sees it as the responsibility of good government to encourage good citizenry but what if the world is just drying up and all the aid in the world won't help the scenario. There are other friends who think that Americans are draining out Canadian lakes. I am not sure how this is done but I do notice water levels change though that might be a rainwater or ecological phenomenon. I am aware of the history of the Los Angeles Aqueduct and how it drained orchard waters to give heft and greater world commerce to what was once the town of San Gabriel.

Could this happen in Ontario, Canada? A drainage of water flow and the catastrophe of food shortages? My friend seems to think it is not far off. His mind has turned very environmental. But does that change things in the larger scheme? Will he even be around regardless of what he does for the posterity of those left after he goes and anything in him that is altruistic enough to leave his land and goods to hordes of the hungry or thirsty rising up from the cities?

If I had more money, I would have more land and grow food for all. I'm not too sure I would have to tell the world about it though. That said, I dig writing a good song that speaks the truth and wants change for the better. Here's to you good friend, to Woody, Bobby Z and all.

Pedro

Pedro, he had himself one last canteen.
There were holes in his shoes and holes in his jeans.
He came to town hungry and angry it seems
but he knew of a farm where they fed all who came
and danced in the fields and danced in the rain
with no fear of famine and slaughter . . .

(to be continued . . .)

WHO IS WHO?
WINSTON CHURCHILL
AND QUANTUM PHYSICS

Small town Ontario. Late fall. Almost Christmas and you can hear the short breath of the wind in this small town. You and your date go into a cafe. Or so it seems. Once inside, you realize it's a dimly lit British pub.

On a stool sits a statue of Winston Churchill. No, wait! It isn't a statue of Winston Churchill; it's a woman who looks like Winston Churchill. Or maybe his sister. But not his dog. Definitely not his dog. You want to move a table so you can cozy up close to a fireplace that's burning warmly and pleasantly. "Can I move the table?" you ask the Winston-Churchill-sister lookalike. "No doll," she replies. You throw a smile around the place which has nothing much to smile at except that you're with an easy-going date and you love British flags. They remind you of The Who.

You were hoping to find a fireplace for you and your date to cozy up to and here it is. But you can't get close enough to it unless you were to do a protest sit-in and wait by the fireplace for the local constabulary to evict you. All you want really is to make the most of the time you have and you've come a long way from the city. Ah, the city—where bar owners let you move a table for the most part unless you plan on taking it outside and throwing it in the back of your car or truck.

Oh well. You go to Plan B: a table where you and your date can both look at the fireplace. You order a coffee and fish and chips. How could that not work in this British flag pub? You wonder what Pete Townshend or Keith Moon would do as you look at the table you were hoping to move. You think: "Yeah, they would maybe smash up the place!"—like auto-destructive art and Gibson guitars and drumkits, leaving it to Roger Daltrey to charm the place. Instead, as your stomach grumbles, you ingest a pale version of fish and chips and coleslaw that is more like cole*slew*. Your date, brave and good-hearted, tucks into her order of lasagna. Terrifically risky in the said environment.

The two of you are being stared at. But you laugh and your date laughs. You think you'd make a good statue. Or maybe this place is really a taxidermist's shop and everything you see is made from the parts of previous customers. And maybe, just maybe the food is too?!—You think about the name of this town—Gram Williams. Who was he? Did he dine here? Is this his Churchill-resembling aunt? You think of the bad old Nazis bombing the Londoners into marmite sandwiches during WW2. But then you think of what the Brits did to Dresden and Chamberlain's acquiescence to Hitleroo and his nasties.

All the while the day is getting darker. Traffic starts to load up the highways home. Where has everyone else been on this cozy late November day? Where are they all going? The red taillights go one way and the headlights go the other. It's getting to look a lot like Christmas. "Maybe she's like Eleanor Rigby," you consider, reflecting yet again on the bar owner. She will live long but really is dying as she is living. Something happened here?! You recall seeing Hitchcock's *Psycho* the day before. And you think: "Of course, that woman — ha — if I had decided to protest and fall asleep on the floor, she might have asked me to milk the cows in the morning, then taxidermied me in the still of night!"

In quantum physics, they say, things change just by looking at them. You see Roger Daltrey sweeping up the bar in the morning. He then sits on a bar stool and waits for the next customer to walk through the door ... "Hello doll ..." You're a statue of an old woman who looks like Winston Churchill's sister. Your date is now a fireplace. She concurs and goes from purr to roar. Outside Keith Moon is heading towards the door, howling and dragging in a haggard-looking Pete Townshend by the arm. You won't get fooled again!

PICKLES AND NASHVILLE

Ah — Bulgarian Cowgirls! Long-legged with big warm eyes. Thus comes a correspondence from country music capital Nashville, TN, with photographs of a certain Olga on my shared music web-site. This site is designed to give opportunity to artists to project their work into social media. Connect artists with each other and allow for the placement of an artist's songs and biography, including upcoming performances and blogs — and a bank should *any viewer want to purchase* one of your compositions.

From the photos, this woman looks like she is real country. Tight jeans, straw cowboy hat curled at the rim and an acoustic six-string guitar flailed over her back as she walks a railroad track looking back at you with her head turned slightly over her shoulder. Lips just a little parted as if singing a tune or saying a soft "Hi."

Wow! Nashville! That's an important town in the scheme of songwriting and music production. You know many local artists in your own hometown but now someone from Nashville wants to let you know how good you are. This correspondence excites your sense of getting your music recognized. You say: "Wow, what I'm creating must be good for me to get a note of congratulations from Nashville—and wow again—from a stunning looking cowgirl!" All a guy could want, right?

But the Bulgarian name lingers a little in the back of your mind. "Isn't that a strange name for a cowgirl country music star? She certainly doesn't look like the Bulgarian, Eastern European women who used to wrestle and weight-lift and throw shot-puts in the Olympic Games. What's Bulgaria got to do with Nashville? you wonder. When you tune in to listen to a sample of her songs, the voice sounds "real country" so you think Olga must be just a bad choice of stage name, given the American south and its star girl names like Dolly, Courtney, Emmy-lou and Loretta. Yeah, what's in a name, anyhow? And look at all the cowboys on stage strumming with her and others drinking beer and raising their glasses in the small club shots? *She's gotta be real!*

You write back a thank you note for becoming a fan on your site. You have put up a few blues oriented songs with a touch of jazz from your latest CD. Very urban blues with lyrics edging on sheer poetry in rhythm and delivery. Almost a lyrical spoken-word jazz rap style. She writes again saying she loves my sound. Her English is perfect as you read the text. Just as in her songs, she seems pretty American as much as you can detect tone in written words, and besides she uses a lot of LOLs and always signs off with)-: or something that's supposed to signify a cheerful cyber-smile. This is very Valley-girl in your mind.

So as she writes telling you how interesting Nashville is, you begin to think that it might be a town you'd like to visit. You give her your personal email as the social media website doesn't allow longer exchanges. In her message she says: "Ola, Hello — It's Olga from Nashville." So you write back and forth a few times and then agree to call each other. She calls first. Tells you she's got these free phone cards that give her special rates almost any time of day. While you are at your desk working one day she calls and a deep Eastern European voice announces that you have to forgive her 'cause she's eating pickles. You are a little taken a-back as you listen to the crunch and slosh and the weight and old country slowness in her voice. Nothing like the pictures she has sent. Nothing like the light country twang in her songs.

As she talks about how high rent is in downtown Nashville, you try to put together the photos and this voice from the other side of where there used to be "The Wall." You keep thinking Colonel Klink and *Hogan's Heroes* and the German and Russian bad guys in all the dramas and comedies you've seen. A little Bela Lugosi with some Marlene Dietrich and Garbo thrown into your ear. But the crunch of pickles brings you back to the moment. "I seeng for da moneey een Sopheeya, but mine man hee's gonned back an' aye trye countrees for da museek. I'm good seenger, you know." "Hmm," you say under your breath. You remember reading about Japanese Karaoke Cowboys but this is different. "Did you like country music in Bulgaria? Or did you just kinda get into it here in North America?" "No, da peeple een Bulgareeya don' like da Western museek. What you call da Countree eh Western Museek dare. I go where I am. Eet's good, you know … I ad- … how do you saye, add-just prettee fine. after da husband leaves." "And now where's your husband? Did he leave for good or do you ever go back to Bulgaria?" I ask. "He's peeg! I don' sleep gud but I seeng. You do da Blues, you know?"

With her last words the phone goes dead. You think to call back but you can't get Dietrich out of your head. The one where she's a sort of Baroness who has a sweet eye for Spencer Tracy and Montgomery Clift has his brain tampered with by the Nazis. And Spencer Tracy "awe shucks" his way through her flattery as he goes to sit as judge on the horrific wars crimes at Nuremberg. You decide that night to go out and rent a movie. You watch and you think of Olga in Nashville. The loneliness. You also think of Nathanael West and *Miss Lonelyhearts*. You think of Montgomery Clift again. His broken nose in the rodeo scene in *The Misfits*. You think of how stiff an actor Clark Gable was.

After the film you play *Return of the Grievous Angel* by Gram Parsons. You hope Olga gets a chance to hear his music along the way. Her beauty stays with you. You might travel to Nashville after all. Maybe you won't and just go on to San Francisco. Just hoping that if you do you won't hear tacky Tony Bennett songs. *White Rabbit* by Grace Slick and the Jefferson Airplane would suit you just fine.

BALL CAP BACKWARDS

*D*a reason I wear da pricetag on my hat
an' ma pants hang down showin' underline line like dat
is da reason I do what I do.
Da reason you're a fool ain't too cool—you go ta school
for all dat tomdickandharry tomfoolery.
Schools—it don't mean %$#@ ta me—get some livin', get some free.
Don't be standing' lookin' at me! You fool! I said—yo!

He made it up on the spot. There I was just coming out of an internet cafe given my home PC went down. A spot outside of my
regular neighbourhood run but I had to stop in and check on
emails and maybe pull up a document or two that had been
attached to Hotmail. I came out for a smoke break and guy was

standing there with his three friends. All of them Hispanic yet he was of African-Canadian descent.

"What's with the price tag?" I ask.

"You gotta smoke?"

"Yeah, but what's with the hat? What do you guys do?"

"Ah, c'mon man! You gotta a smoke for me and my friends?"

"Sure. You guys into music?"

"Rap, man. C'mon, gimme a smoke. Whadda you do?"

"Sing. Write songs. Poems. Here."

He moves in close for a light as that's something he needs too. His friends want smokes all around and I light them all up.

"What kind of songs, man?"

"I could do one for you. The words anyway."

"Shoot!" he says pointing his index finger, holding the smoke to his mouth and tilting his ear in.

Just when you thought the thing would run
slow in the dancing confound of love
you realized a note, forgotten, expansive
on its own ...

"%&$*—man!" he interrupts before I finish the verse. "What's that %&$*?"

"You do any?" I ask.

"Ha haha—ha—me? Yeah, we do. Gimme another smoke man—one more ppleaaase man?

He reaches to grab the pack from my hand and as I swipe his hand away, he sways back, his cap falling off his head. A full pack of smokes in its cup.

SMART-ASS TALK

(*Independence Day* versus *On The Road*)

Will Smith smokes a cigar with Jeff Goldblum. They are about to run an explosive device into an intruding alien, mother spacecraft and give us all that sense of sacrifice and survival against forces so set on destroying humanity.

Sal Paradise sits on the roof of his run down jalopy in the midst of a Mexican/Guatemalan jungle and says to himself the ecstasy of the bugs landing on his body in a steam of dense sweat makes him reflect on the richness of the country-side and the beauty of the woman whom he meets at a Tijuana bus-stop, whom he has made love to a few chapters back.

Characters in both *Independence Day* and *On the Road* are buddy-travelling. In the former, all will be understood and resolved by the smart-ass courage of the protagonists—America and the rest of the dumb world will be saved by American Cowboy bravado and spunk dressed in fighter-pilot and hip scientist mode. In *On the Road*, the narrator Paradise through his travels with Moriarty finds the underside, the marginalized, the destitute, the hungry in the country, small towns and cities, and celebrates every moment of non-conventionality. Half living in criminality. Dean Moriarty talks hip. He is seeking knowledge and so is Sal. They do not know what their adventure will be.

On the other hand, Goldblum and Smith know exactly what their adventure is and we do too. You can't miss it with all the stars and stripes and melodramatic hyperbole of a musical score. And it's all designed properly (that is to say politically correct) as there are the African-Americans digging the whites who happen to be President (Caucasian) and Scientist (Jewish). And predictably, the African-Americans are either nurse or fighter pilot (service jobs). Interestingly though both fighter pilot (Smith) and President speak in heroic platitudes about the state of the world and the get-up-and-go it's gonna take to beat back the alien foe. And his smart-ass talk is at its height in a previous scene with Smith dissin' the aliens as he drags one back in his parachute to the lab for all the smart-ass scientists and politicians to analyze. (It is interesting that this film was made on the back of the 9/11 attacks on American soil. Un-subtle rhetoric and jingoism is one of American film-makers' go to themes for big dollars.)

Sal (Kerouac) is taken by Moriarty's (Neal Cassady) constant quest and need for movement. Moriarty is a marginal character if you were to view him in society at large. Petty car thief, stealing his way into every woman's bedroom, getting his nose broken and half drunk, bennied-up through most of the book. But to Sal he is a "saint." The Saint of the Road, and action, able to withstand anything the road throws at him and say "give me more." His smart-ass talk does not pretend to solve the woes of a country. The writer (Kerouac) intends for Moriarty to only be all that he is and his ruddy and tough enthusiasm infects Sal's quest for meaning in life through movement. I.e.: Movement *is* meaning in *On the Road*.

If one was to play a bit of interspersing of narratives and put Dean Moriarty and Will Smith in the cockpit of an alien jet attacking the mother ship, Dean might say something akin to: "Yaz! Yaz! We're gonna ball this Jack!" And Smith might return with: "Damn! Let's do it!!" There indeed would be a kinship. The differences however in the creators' intents stand out. Smith represents triumph before it triumphs with flaring machismo and a loving wife that supports it. Even a President who is saved by this jingoistic swagger. Kerouac's Moriarty just wants to keep going. He could probably live on the alien ship or planet and explore, befriend and "dig it," whereas Smith would be cursing it as though tattooed to an ever-lasting umbilical cord twined in red-white-and blue-ism.

Two different modes of travel with signs along the way. One smart-ass exploring the road (America) and the other beating up aliens that don't even exist but for the fear factor in post-9/11 America that the film-makers were most happy to exploit. The difference between fiction (*On the Road*) and sci-fi hyperbolic fantasy. The difference between a quest for involvement and exploring the unknown (Moriarty) and an expression of crushing the unknown or naming the unknown as evil and "alien." And the manifestation of superiority in the world — *Independence Day*. Both American, but one less superficial in narrative and characterization than the other. To Moriarty's "Ball that Jack?" Will Smith might say: "What country you from, man? This is America!"

I CAN'T GET NO SATISFACTION AND DARKNESS AT THE BREAK OF NOON AND GINSBERG'S HOWL

(Poetry and only the *Suggestion* of it)

U rban. Dark. Nuclear. The standing of the spirit against urbanity's curse. Advertising. The hypocrisy of a system that takes away all aspects of individuality. And in contrarianism lies the key to identity. Bobby Z. Dylan sings *It's Alright Ma (I'm Only Bleeding)* aiming his voice from what feels and seems like one of the most alienating mornings, afternoons or evenings New York City can muster up. The choice he makes is to not cave to the overwhelming barrage of capitalist driven miasma of the surrounding urban landscape and its effect on the spirit. He chooses attack.

And in the attack there is no lack of poetry, as much as a song can carry poetry, and even change the nature of poetry or add to its force. The long lines and phrasing, a distinct influence of both

Allen Ginsberg's *Howl* and Kerouac's prose, brings "an idea" of jazz vernacular to simple oral/folk music rhythms. The voice never hesitates, nor does it lilt in full rests but there is a warning in the half-breaths that a truth is being spoken. That if not having to be heard, at least has to get out before the writer can move on.

The poetry? A maturity in song lyric unknown but maybe for the works of Bertolt Brecht with the accompanying music of Kurt Weill. Taking on the forces that create oppression in life though Bobby Z's attack is more a defence than a full out alternative to surviving society's constraints. Unlike The Rolling Stones' *Satisfaction*, *It's Alright Ma* has lyrical depth and length that moves it out of pop-song category. Nothing like either appeared before 1965 though both show the range of song that became popular as the decade progressed. At one end (The Stones) with their hard edge and often Motown-influenced Blues, releasing a three minute pop rush articulating an almost James Dean-like stance of "nothing that has been presented to me works for my generation" (my interpretation). At the other end, Bobby Z with a ferocity and velocity of image and percussive acoustic guitar, articulates what to avoid, not in a grand political quest for re-evaluating "society's pliers" but a path for his own individual freedom, from society's hypocrisies and constraints.

Though both *It's Alright Ma* and *Satisfaction* seem to come from the displeased new generation of youth, Bobby Z's articulation is more akin to the "angry young man" literature and play-writing of late 1950s British Theatre. By their articulation they re-shaped the cultural landscape. They are saying that what has worked for previous generations, doesn't work for them. And as The Stones' song has an aspect of posing to it, its full-blooded extension is Bobby Z's richer articulation. This trait and the long lines and verses give *It's Alright Ma* a poetry that many other songs of the era only suggest. With Bobby Z we have true poetry set to music. With other songs of the period, we have music with lyric that suggest poetry but really isn't outside of its own context and, let's say, only carries poetic intent.

There is no real vision in *Satisfaction*. Nor is there really insight. *It's Alright Ma* has both vision and insight and celebrates the individual's perception. And in an uncanny way, articulates a joy that society's constraints and hypocrisies can be detected and named. "Moloch" from Allen Ginsberg's seminal beat poem *Howl* comes to mind. Moloch, the Sanskrit god who demands high sacrifice and symbolizes the causes of ruin — (as Ginsberg intended the metaphor for capitalism). And in turn, Dylan finds continuum in the voice against capitalism's corruptive forces. *What sphinx of cement and aluminum bashed open their skulls and ate up their brains and imagination?* says Ginsberg's *Howl*, while Dylan's *It's Alright Ma* says: *Advertising signs they con / you into thinkin' you're the one / that can do what's never been done / that can win what's never been won / meantime life outside goes on / all around you.*

So as The Stones' *Satisfaction* hints at alienation and articulates aspects of youthful anger, it does not contain the maturity of the individual voice against corrupting forces in a studied, timeless and archetypical manner. Great, visceral pop-song that *Satisfaction* is, Dylan in his work of the same period (mid 1960s), finds the fusion of popular culture (rock music) and high culture (poetry), which *Satisfaction* only hints at and suggests. And Mr. Bobby Z. sets a poetic-lyric standard, if not for himself, for other musician-songwriters to aspire to, or take note of.

TITLES

What titles do is embrace and suggest, say it all in a phrase or word. Make you want to open a book or allow you to recall a song or work of art. Kings and Queens have titles. So do judges and ministers in various forms of government. Titles do what a full text cannot do. One bad title can be firing-squad time. It is hard to recover from a book with a bad title. They can take forever to come up with or come in a flash and flood as if from prophetic skies.

The titles for these segments run the gamut. From simple — "The Internet Café" to "World Cup Jazz" — a bit more suggestive of something that may in fact never happen and needs a name. For the most part these titles came in through the early spring air (mid-autumn as I write this), as I walked out for my early a.m.

espresso. As a songwriter I have always thought that once you have a title you are half-way (and sometimes more) on the way home. I had no intent to have these come. It was a dreary day of chilly April with no sign of clearing skies in sight.

But like a good poem or song, the titles kept coming (almost in separate lines) with rhythm and clarity. Ringing the typewriter bell here and there. So I imagined the titles being filled not on a computer monitor but a typewriter. The beauty of a typewriter is that it allowed mistakes and you can hear them. And not being one to go back over text in the immediate moment or time and time again, the actual typos or thoughts of them before I began, sort of gave me a free run. I knew I had to go back, 'cause my typing skills ended with Mrs. Wegg in grade ten. Mrs. Wegg had halitosis and that in turn gave my fingers some accuracy as I had trouble with her stopping over me for long.

There could have been more titles but my guitar called me thus I offer these few pages as not more than the momentum of thought and perception and what Roland Barthes called "writing degree zero." Titles? Titles are like a name given to you. Yet unlike a birth name they are selected usually by one parent. Not that all writers or artists are parents and certainly not vice versa. A bad title can sink a work of art or make it sound like there's nothing else you'd need to do but let the folks down at the local cafes know the title to the latest novel or movie you've read or seen.

Titles are enough to make you buy a product advertised on TV or through other media. Make you wanna buy a mop or kitchen gloves or that great automobile of your dreams or needs. Even mortgage purchases have nifty titles. And the people at the bank called "financial officers" as if they are in charge of the Brink's truck and aren't merely tellers. Even the banks are called "financial institutions." A bit of vanity I suppose. To think of that little corner bank as though it was The World Monetary Fund or Treasury

Department. Without language and its capacity to evoke, re-invent and create images in this manner, you don't get titles.

You can have titles changed. I.e.: What might have been called "The Main Street Subway Station" could be sold to ITA Insurance and those too old to take in the new name may get lost in their later years when needing assistance as their memory for short term 'items' fades. Value? Why not name some of the stations "The Picasso Lady," "The Sunflowers," "The Remington," "The Jacques Louis David"? Because those painters are dead and gone and there is no money to be made by *artistic squatting.* Or you could name the stations after parts of the body. "The Heart Station," "The Elbow," "The Kneeling Station"? Although the latter would certainly not work in a dominantly Protestant town. Or historical titles? "The Civil War Station," "The Hastings Station." "Twin Towers Central." Or even better still, after great rock & roll songs? "Stairway to Heaven Station" (don't even need the article). "Rolling Stone Station" (not to be confused with the magazine). But the best would be "Vanity Park." We need some mavericks in our cultural soup to get some language into the soul of the grey and whiteness of urbanity.

Why are reality TV shows called "*reality*" TV? Most people I talk to who are aware or have tried to watch them call it @#&*! Poets seems to come up with good titles even though some of their poems are pretty bad. A great title and great poem is "The Wasteland." A good title and bad poem is "I Have No More Bananas For Sale," about a man who sees his task as moving up the society ladder from fruit-stand vendor to marketing genius. And to give a place or product a foreign name seems to have been a wonder. I mean, how could you not want to purchase the latest automobile named "Le Car"? So elusive in its poetic suggestion. Or the latest film (make that movie) titled, *Le Movie*?

One wonders that as language seems to spiral downwards whether there is a part of our cultural lexicon that is spiralling upwards? And where would that be occurring? It is hard to imagine a title like "The Immune Face of Gravity" with its new-age-like, semi-platitudinal syntax as being one. Though the title might suggest lightness, the pedantic strophes leave you nothing but earthbound. Take too *The Unbearable Lightness of Being*. It always feels like there should be another word at the end of this title. Maybe, "The Unbearable Lightness of Being *Me*, or *Sam* or *Jane?*" Perhaps the title is more poetic in its native Czech? One title you can't mess with much is *The Inferno*. Italian, Latin or English, the title's *clear as hell* and its gonna come off. To translate the title as "Hell" would bring it down, though the full title of his opus *The Divine Comedy* sounds decent in English, but certainly more powerful and sweeping as *La Divina Commedia* in Italian.

No Logo by Canadian author Naomi Klein is a good title. Nothing better than no name and the capacity to mean something. *Tenth Avenue Freeze-Out* by Bruce Springsteen on his *Born to Run* album from the mid-'70s was a good title. On the other hand, *Born in the U.S.A.* was not. Its intent might have been clear but its irony wasn't. Some titles are hilarious from the top and you just want to say them. *Dead Skunk in the Middle of the Road* by New England songwriter Loudon Wainright III (great name) comes to mind. A country singer from Canada's capital, Ottawa, had a fantastic country-twang tune titled *You've Got Sawdust on the Floor of Your Heart*, squeezing out and satirizing the genre's need for melodramatic expression.

Band names come to light as well. Who the hell are "The Trews"? Who cares? "The Who" kicks ass! "The Guess Who" does not, and did little service to the great compositions of Randy Bachman and Burton Cummings. I would have thought to name them "Guess." Then we have the literate British bands. "Pink Floyd," "Jethro Tull," "Led Zeppelin" on up to "Dire Straits" and "The Clash." "The Beatles" is a name that doesn't serve the great nature and growth of the seminal band from Northern England.

Sports teams? This is where it gets racy, (if not racist) to some. "Cleveland Indians." "Washington Redskins." "Edmonton Eskimos." "Atlanta Braves" (though I'm sure there are brave white men in Atlanta). And the coolest names like "Utah Jazz," "Miami Heat," "Orlando Magic" and "Phoenix Sun." And the mediocre ones like "Blue Jays" (what a threat!), "Diamondbacks" and "Padres." Two of the best are "New York Yankees" and "The Montreal Canadiens" with the 'e' instead of the Anglo 'a'. Truly a hometown team by cultural and geographical intent, as are "The New York Yankees." As for logos (visual titles) "The Detroit Redwings" (winged wheel) though it is meant to symbolize the motor city, brings a sense of classical mythology by its use of a wing and wheel as in chariots and Pegasus and Mercury. This is all by suggestion.

"The Edmonton Oilers," having produced one of the greatest hockey players (Wayne Gretzky), is a fairly ho-hum title even though it identifies that the team is from Alberta. A glance back at the titles above sure says the National Basketball Association is ahead of the pack in the name and title game.

Then there are names given to products. "Mr. Clean" seems right enough. But what is "Viagra" supposed to mean? "Pepsodent" was clear but "Colgate" sounds like you are about to do something heavy and nuclear to your teeth. "Dentyne" is cool with the "y" but "Trident" sounds like you could end up resembling a walrus with tusks if you used it. It also suggests you may only have three teeth trolling the depths of the sea.

NASA had great names from the sixties onwards. Mercury, Apollo, Jupiter, Columbia and Challenger until it crossed the line with a space shuttle named "Enterprise," drawing from the *Star Trek* TV series. "The Wrath of Khan" however is a super and loaded title. You get John Steinbeck and Genghis Khan in the same breath.

The significance of titles and names fills out our plumes. We puff up when called by them and allow words to define (as best we can) the five senses' need for allusion and indication. Everything doesn't need to be called something but *we* need to call *it* something. We can't hang out with a preposition. What was *IT*, speaking of products? Something that whitened nurses' shoes and tennis sneakers. Prepositions for the most part don't make good names or titles. Then the other extreme. The gangsters of America. Lucky, Pretty-Boy, Baby-Face, Scarface, Bugsy. FBI identifiers. The noun and adjective arrive together here. And certainly Disney's "Seven Dwarfs" (not Dwarves) indicated an aspect of psychology as if the *seven* names given them suggest the luckiest number on the face of thrown dice. Why seven? Was Walt a gambler and coming with seven, waking up from an all-nighter?

Back to musical acts for a moment. Would Garfunkel and Simon have worked? Don't think so. Sounds like possibly piano or carpet repairmen or sellers. And then again, The Who with its collection of best songs titled *Meaty, Beaty, Big and Bouncy*—the sexual suggestion outweighed by the four members of the band looking street and rowdy to match their elaborate power chords. Then there are the one name acts. Donovan. That works. Jewel doesn't. Too precious. But then after the unfortunate deaths of some of rock & roll's best, we had Janis, Jim, Jimi, all on a first name basis. And Elvis? The name is unusual enough. Well, certainly was to the American northeast, including New York City. But when you say Elvis 'Presley', somehow there's church music from small town America in it. Then there's John Mellencamp. Great, almost football name. Had to start out as Johnny Cougar, then managed to get it to John Cougar Mellencamp. Then managed to get rid of his manager and write some of the best Americana of the '70s, '80s and '90s.

And then back to poetry. The finest of American contemporary poetry came from John Ashbery's *Self-Portrait in a Convex Mirror* in reference to Giotto, the Renaissance painter renowned for drawing the perfect free-hand circle. And *Howl* by Beat poet Allen Ginsberg! How hard to beat is that?! And *Bomb* from Gregory Corso in reaction to nuclear bomb escalation during the Cold War.

And so titles and names run the gamut. Good. Bad. Too long. Too short. Too lingering and double-entendrish to a fault. Clever by a half. Racist. Derogatory. Emancipating. Enlightening. Evocative. Sexy. Drab. Foreign. Ill-grammar-ed (in a good way). Bad-grammar-ed in a subtle way and good-grammar-ed in a terrible, monotonous manner. And that's without seeing a piece of artwork or hearing the tune or reading the verse or prose or getting to the ballpark or rink and living past your birth name. Filling out the name's possibility. A title is like a name you give your kid with hope. Vanity too. But a title or name isn't as clear as a birthmark. Regardless, happy birthday to all! Whether there are many candles or few and your name gets spelled "write" on the bakery product!

IN MEMORIAM

(Full Moon Lou)

I t's a full moon and there ain't no Lou. It's been forty-some years and there ain't no Jim. New York. L.A. Baseball's done for the year and hockey's pushing a quarter of the way in. Concussions abound and bullies continue to win. The sky's missing colour. The night sky, that is. The sky when you walk the downtown and look for and feel for that extra dimension. That song that you wake with in the middle of the night or a dream that tells you something somewhere is alive beyond these hanging tree limbs and neons selling it all always.

My first real Lou was '89. The *New York* CD. On a Dutch yacht in Georgian Bay and the crescent stillness of the boat swinging back and forth in the summer full moonlight. My film-maker friend, Bill, had just scored a small fortune doing the first exposé on the Soviet space program post-empire. And he bought a yacht. But first he bought a Mercedes. "You wanna have lunch?" he called one cold-ass February morning. "Yeah sure. Let's get out otherwise we die doing nothing on these freezer-from-hell days," I responded.

So Bill came by and said: "You heard this?" as he slipped a CD into his new-fan-dangled sound-system. LIGHT MY FIRE — LIGHT MY FIRE — LIGHT MY FIRE — YEAH YEAH! LIGHT MY FIRE — LIGHT MY FIRE — LIGHT MY FIREYAH — YEAAHHHH — UUUUUH! "Where you wanna eat?' Bill asked. "I don't know — maybe Mars?" I suggested. But the food didn't matter. Just getting out on a day of dark drizzle did. Proved there was life. And it had been years since Coppola's *Apocalypse Now* with that poster of Brando's face and a dragonfly moon helicopter riding the sky above it. And if the napalm fire wasn't enough you had 'The End' at the beginning. Genius and high metaphor at work. No Godfather in-jokes. We're talkin' real American shit here! The drudge and drag of a screwed-up war!

The aftermath left for film-makers and artists to give some sense to through an image here and an image there. The senselessness and madness — and Jim saw it all real young. From the 1966 "If You Go Out in the Woods Tonight"-like eerieness of *People are Strange* to his Kinks-like *Hello I Love You,* Jim lit it up early and exhaled all the Rimbaud a rock poet could muster up. Then, on a road crew in the middle of country-road-nowhere dusk one summer, with the red tail-lights of cars and trucks in the dimming distance, what comes out of the radio but "There's a killer on the road . . ." with the piano like rain and the sizzle of cooling just-laid asphalt filling the air. My impression at the time was — "@#$% — it's scary out there beyond making a buck to pay for university fees. This ain't merely about pop music and Sergeant Pepper and Beach Boy steals of Chuck Berry riffs. This is serious @#$#!" And it felt like Jim wanted to live but not at the cost of not dying if that's what it took to make life worth living.

And Lou. Mister full moon shining his face in the corners where you don't sleep. Or do in what seems like comfort, and think the bad bad world is far away. Given the present day context of pre-meditated vulgarity chefs, steroid-clad baseballers and film celebrities with yellow journalists following them, and looking back, Lou kicked more than ass at the un-hip underbelly within American culture in his time. He kicked his own soul around New York and made New York feel like it was no further than a turn-table's spin away. And the calm! — *Walk On the Wild Side*'s most intriguing aspect is the non-panic vocal. Like it all goes down cool. And though the voice suggests a hint of judgment, it isn't judgment as much as assessing and giving authoritative perspective from the inside to those who are outside it all.

On the other hand — it's a whisper to insiders (one of which you oddly feel like) about what New York feels at night. It's that *whisp-er*. Not a saxophone and not a clarinet. Maybe a bit more akin to subtle jazz brushes on a soft snare shuffling through the streets. That's Lou's voice. And it's in that "Doo-doo doo — doo doo doo doo doo ..." telegraph signal of his vocal chords! And *The Sword of Damocles* from *Magic and Loss* — like this guy was smarter than your classical mythology professor. And that sword dangling above your head — telling you a little something about greed and destiny and the power and pains of being either a poor man or a king. This is something Iggy and Bowie didn't do. Re-deliver ancient truths within rock & roll's modalities. Stretch rock & roll to its literary limits. If in fact, there are any limits.

A music Artists and Repertoire friend once compared rock & roll bands to Luigi Pirandello's *Six Characters in Search of an Author*. He said: "You listen to that stuff and you can change folks around — like Jimi Hendrix coulda been in Cream and Hank Williams coulda been in the Eagles and so on ... just mix 'em all around." "What's the Pirandello part?" I asked intrigued. "You know—if you're like a mogul like Geffen—well look what he did with Crosby, Still Nash and Young?" "Yeah but the characters revolt some in Pirandello—don't like their roles. Seems to me CSNY were kind of copasetic—no?" "Yeah, yeah, but to make it work at the bank, for me, you gotta have the power to move them around. But there's two guys I couldn't move with a bulldozer." "Who? I asked. "Lou. You can't move Lou and you can't move Jim."

And to paraphrase that abundantly beat and lonesome traveller Kerouac Jack, from days-gone-by to this age-gone-dog, if he were alive today, and dug some Underground and Doors:

So in this Hemisphere when the moon goes down, I sit at one of those urban all night-into-the-morning cafes, watching short short skies below the skyscrapers and low-rises and sense the big turntables turning and the roadies setting up from stadium to stadium from L.A. to New York and all north and south and east and west and in between. And I know there must be a lot of kids who aren't sleeping. Listening to their muse—iPadding and YouTubing where G(god) ain't no Pooh Bear (or Poobah) and the final shore ain't a shore at all but a long ether cable cyberspacing us together—and I think of Lou and Jim, cutting the continent in half and going to Paris and Berlin—I think of Jim and Lou. I think of Lou and Jim.

ABOUT THE AUTHOR

Joseph Maviglia is a singer-songwriter, poet and essayist whose work has appeared in journals and media across North America and Europe. His tribute poem *jazz dharma* was commissioned by CBC's *The Sunday Edition* to commemorate the 50th anniversary of Alan Ginsberg's iconic poem *Howl*. His latest CD is *Angel in the Rain*, and his song *Father, It's Time* appeared on the Juno Award-winning compilation *The Gathering*. His composition, *Calabresella/ Sooner or Later*, is featured in the film *The Resurrection of Tony Gitone*. A selection of his poetry will be published in Italy in the anthology *A Nord del Sogno (North of the Dream)*. A collection of his poetry, *A God Hangs Upside Down*, was published by Guernica. He is presently working on a new collection of songs for a soon-to-be released CD.

RECYCLED
Paper made from
recycled material
FSC® C100212

Printed in February 2014
by Gauvin Press,
Gatineau, Québec